HEARTSTONE

A journey out of the midnight of my soul

TIM YOUNG

HYBIGINEE BOOKS

HEARTSTONE

Copyright © 2009 by Tim Young. All rights reserved.

No part of this publication may reproduced, stored in or introduced into a retrieval system, or transmitted, in any form or by any means (electronic, mechanical, photocopying, recording or otherwise), without the prior written permission from the author. The scanning, uploading, and distribution of this book via the Internet or via any other means without the permission of the author is illegal and punishable by law. Please purchase only authorized electronic editions and do not participate in or encourage electronic piracy of copyrightable materials. Your support of the author's rights is appreciated.

Scripture taken from THE MESSAGE. Copyright © by Eugene H. Peterson 1993, 1994, 1995, 1996, 2000, 2001, 2002. Used by permission of NavPress Publishing Group.

Scripture taken from the Holy Bible, New International Version ®. Copyright © 1973, 1978, 1984 International Bible Society. Used by permission of Zondervan. All rights reserved.

Scripture quotations marked "NKJV™" are taken from the New King James Version®. Copyright © 1982 by Thomas Nelson, Inc. Used by permission. All rights reserved.

Holy Bible, New Living Translation, copyright © 1996, 2004, 2007 by Tyndale House Foundation. Scripture quotations marked (NLT) are taken from the Holy Bible, New Living Translation, copyright © 1996, 2004, 2007. Used by permission of Tyndale House Publishers, Inc., Carol Stream, Illinois 60188. All rights reserved.

All references to the works of Oswald Chambers taken from My Utmost for His Highest, (c) 1992 by Oswald Chambers Publications Association, Ltd. Original Edition. (c) l935 by Dodd Mead & Co., renewed (c) 1963 by the Oswald Chambers Publications Assn., Ltd., and is used by permission of Barbour Publishing, Uhrichsville, Ohio. All rights reserved.

Please take note that I chose not to capitalize the name satan and related names, as I chose not to acknowledge him, even to the point of violating grammatical rules.

http://heartstonejourney.com

Original project title 'Held by Grace'
Cover image: On the summit, © Jackie Egginton | Dreamstime.com
Edited by Wendy Jo Dymond

ISBN 978-1449976286
LCCN 2010901129

Printed in the United States of America

חירות

For Danae and Joshua.
May this journey inspire you!

The prudent see danger and take refuge, but the simple keep going and suffer for it.
Proverbs 27:12 (NIV)

Acknowledgments

With special thanks to

- the many people God has placed in my life that have had an impact on me and, directly or indirectly, have enabled me to share this story.
- Doug Banks, who personally pursued this project with me, providing the much needed guidance and editorial review.
- Wendy Jo Dymond, who did an amazing job with the final editing of Heartstone.
- Rick and Debra Evans, Ivan and Brenda Maillet, Scott Feffer, Janine Carmilia-Smith, Mark Warren, and many others for helping me with review and commentary.
- Rick and Debra Evans, who walked with me into the dark places in my heart.
- The Oswald Chambers Publications Association Ltd. (http://oswaldchambers.co.uk) for their kind permission to reference the works of Oswald Chambers.
- My Dad and Pat, who provided the resources for the final editing of Heartstone.
- My mom, dad, and sister, whom I love very much.
- My Lord and Savior, Jesus Christ, who gets all the glory for this book!

Contents

ACKNOWLEDGMENTS IV

PREFACE VII

FOREWORD VIII

INTRODUCTION IX

FIRST STONE § WALLS 1

CHOICES 2
FRACTURED 11
ALONE 15
DIVINE ONENESS 18
HARDSHIP 22
WOUNDS 29
CRY 33
RISE 36

SECOND STONE § MOUNTAINS 40

CLARITY 41
WAVES 48
SYMBOLS 51
THE FOUR STONES 52

THIRD STONE § WILDERNESS 59

DELAYS 60
TEST 64
CORNERS 68
PRODIGAL 73
STUMBLES 78
MY HIDING PLACE 83
RIPPLES 87

COLLISION	93
BETHESDA	98
STILL	102
SURRENDER	105
STRENGTH	110

FOURTH STONE § PROMISED LAND 112

SIGNPOSTS	113
STRONGHOLDS	118
THE BATTLE	123
JUMP	128
WINEPRESS	133
KNEES	139
JARS	142
CONFRONTATION	146
NIGHTSONG	152
PSALMS 73 [MY VERSION]	156
HOPE	158
TEARS	160
REMEMBER	165

NOTES 169

PREFACE

I know very well how foolish the message of the cross sounds to those who are on the road to destruction. But we who are being saved recognize this message as the very power of God.
1 Corinthians 1:18 (NLT)

What story is your life telling? Is it a mess? Is it lonely and difficult?

I don't want to presume to know what your situation may or may not be, but I can tell you that there is a God who can and will restore the years life has stolen from you. If Heartstone has any message that can resonate with you it is that "You are not alone!"

Come and take a journey with me through the pages of my personal failure, defeat, lost expectations, and my final devastation. Heartstone is a story about a people who faced the giants that we all face, and the keys God gave them (and has given each of us) to deal with those giants and turn theirs and our broken solitude into a field of dreams.

The truth of God's word is that He has already written the story of your life. It is time for you to read that story and find your road home. God's truth is that He has a plan for you that is good and not for evil. A plan where you win in the end. Let Heartstone be the beginning of your journey home. This time the happy ending will be your own.

He wants you to have a beautiful ending!

Foreword

Life can often present us with circumstances we never anticipated. The unfortunate truth is that we all have to navigate these difficult seasons with little understanding, not much experience, and a willingness to learn more about ourselves than we wanted to know.

Tim Young has given us a transparent view, through *Heartstone*, outlining many of these moments in his own life, with the hope that his chronicled journey will enlighten our own.

This book is more than a good read, a gift for a hurting friend, or an outline of someone else's life with another happy ending; it is a resource for daily life, with lessons that go beyond any individual circumstance. Debra and I are thrilled to recommend both the book and the author to you.

Rick and Debra Evans
www.livinginfaith.com
www.411impact.com

Introduction

"Hey, Dad, God has been inviting me to make another climb up Mt. Lafayette. His invitation is an all-consuming nudge that I can't escape, and I was wondering if you would put aside your plans for Saturday and take the journey with me." Knowing that this was my Mount Horeb, my dad put his plans aside, curiously excited to go on adventure and take this hike with his son.

We woke up early that morning of July 4, 2008; gathered our hiking gear; jumped in the car; and headed north to the White Mountains of New Hampshire. Before driving too far, we decided that it would be a great idea to make a quick detour to get a caffeine boost at the nearest Dunkin' Donuts. My eyes were still adjusting from the transition of darkness to light as the sun began to peek over the horizon when I lowered my coffee cup to share with my dad a thought that had popped into my head. "You know, Dad, it's been four years since I made this climb, when God asked me to pick up four stones and bring them down the mountain with me. Remember how these four stones have become a binding theme in my life and guideposts along my journey with God?" My dad continued the conversation by replaying the events of these past four years and admitted his excitement and curiosity when I asked him to join me on this hike. We were both very eager to see what adventures God had in store for us on this climb.

On our drive to the mountain, the jet stream of life slowly faded into the background as I became immersed in the much-needed conversation with my dad. The pull focus was retelling the story of the four stones and all the adventures I experienced during these four years after my divorce. The depth of this conversation was something that I craved growing up so I soaked up every word, every emotion I could, during our time together.

Approaching Franconia Notch from the south is like entering a different world. It doesn't take long to see the prominent protrusion of the Whitney-Gilman ridge with the Black Dike in its shadow as Cannon Mountain approaches. Passing exit 34A (the Flume), we headed for the "Trailhead Parking" sign which came into clear view after passing the Basin, a granite pothole twenty feet in diameter smoothed out by small stones and sand whirled around by the Pemigewasset River. As we pulled into the parking lot, we were welcomed by a crystal-clear sky and steady, but soft morning breeze. We geared up and decided to retrace the steps of my last journey as we began our ascent to the summit via the Bridle Path trail.

Up the mountain we went.

After hiking a while, we were relieved to see the Greenleaf Appalachian Mountain Club (AMC) hut coming into view, as we were ready for some lunch before our final ascent. In July, the hut opens each day to serve weary, hungry hikers freshly baked bread, homemade lemonade, and a warm, delicious tomato soup. It was really nice to shed our backpacks and boots as we rejuvenated our tired bodies with a hot lunch and more great conversation.

"Hey, Dad, wouldn't it be awesome to find the same large rock that I stood on during my last journey? You know…the place where God and I had a conversation about the four stones?" My dad simply answered by encouraging me to ask God to lead us to it. As we continued our hike toward the summit I did just that and asked God to lead us to the exact spot. There was no way we could find the exact location on our own because the terrain started looking the same.

As we neared the summit, a noticeable wind came out of nowhere ushering our steps in a direction that took us off the marked path we were on. We wandered in what seemed to be the wrong direction, and it wasn't long before the familiar marker of the large rock came into focus. I found myself again standing upon this awe-inspiring centerpiece in the vast exposed area of the mountain. Standing there on the rock, I took a deep breath, lifted my head to the Heavens and began to have another conversation with God.

The wind blows wherever it pleases. You hear its sound, but you cannot tell where it comes from or where it is going. So it is with everyone born of the Spirit. —John 3:8 (NIV)

Stepping down from the rock, my dad ran over to me. Before he could ask me what happened, I said, "God told me that He has placed a heart-shaped stone within the ruins of the hotel foundation on the summit." My dad looked at me somewhat bewildered, but remembering my last conversation with God here, he decided to just come along for the ride.

Our already sore feet carried us quickly to the summit, matching step for step with the anxious beating of my heart. Greeted by the ruins of an old hotel foundation I began my prayer walk within the crumbling walls to discover a heart shaped stone. It took some time, but I faithfully pursued it, placing my complete trust in the words He spoke to me. Like a little child on Christmas morning, I ran over to my dad with an overflowing joy to show him. "Dad, check this out, I found it. I found the heartstone!"

The Spirit of God moves with a mystery we cannot understand. He influences whatever He wants, where, when, on whom, and in what measure and degree, He pleases. His soft winds led me to the base of Mt. Lafayette, my own Mount Horeb, to once again make the ascent to the mountaintop to encounter the living God. His soft winds guided my steps again to the large rock hidden on the mountain. His soft winds led me to the heartstone that God had placed within the walls of the hotel ruin.

Four years ago, He led me to discover four stones. Today, He has led me to find one:—His heartstone.

Restoration.

Somehow we come to a place on our journey where we find ourselves completely lost, without direction, in valleys of life where we finally come to the end of ourselves and we want to come home. The "somehow" became a reality in my life when the crisis of divorce beat me down to the place where I desperately wanted to come home, and my heart was willing. He has been pursuing me with the soft winds of His Spirit through all the hurts, pain, sorrows, and disappointments. Through these journeys, He has healed my heart, and it has been restored.

> The Holy Spirit is determined that we will have the realization of Jesus Christ in every area of our lives, and He will bring us back to the same point over and over again until we do.—Oswald Chambers

I remember holding the four fragmented pieces of stone in my hands on this mountaintop four years ago, not fully understanding the significance that these symbols would represent in my life. Today I stand here on this very same mountaintop holding a heartstone in my hand…a heartstone that is not broken, a heartstone that has been beautifully restored, a heartstone to remind me that it is in His nearness that there is healing and that everything broken is made whole and restored in its fullness.

What story is your life telling?

Mine? I invite you to walk with me through these pages as I share my story, my journey. Take no more with you than the question, "Can God take the clutter of my life, with everything seemingly stacked against it and redeem it?"

I offer you only my story; walk with me…

> If you can meet with Triumph and Disaster, and treat those two impostors just the same… —Rudyard Kipling

First Stone § Walls

They told me, "The exile survivors who are left there in the province are in bad shape. Conditions are appalling. The wall of Jerusalem is still rubble; the city gates are still cinders." When I heard this, I sat down and wept. I mourned for days, fasting and praying before the God-of-Heaven. —Nehemiah 1:3, 4 (MSG)

Circumstances may appear to wreck our lives and God's plans, but God is not helpless among the ruins. Our broken lives are not lost or useless. God comes in and takes the calamity and uses it victoriously, working out His wonderful plan of love.—
—Eric Lidell

Choices

"I am working on a major project that requires my time right now, and it's really important and strategic to the company. I will have to work late again tonight. I'm sorry, but the company needs me right now. Can you leave my dinner in the microwave and tell the kids that I love them before you put them to bed?" Distracted as I hang up the phone, I slip back into my blind devotion to the needs of the company, convincing myself that I am really doing this for my family so I can provide a better life for them.

Looking for my value, my self-worth, and my identity with position and success, I would always choose a safe retreat into my hiding place of counterfeit affirmation—selling my soul to my work. Receiving the glory of man through the recognition of another successful project; earning more money; advancing to that next, higher title on the corporate ladder, I continued to retreat from the pain and insecurities of my fractured life, protecting my empire as I chased my American dream with a blind devotion. The dream of this empire was something I wanted so badly that I failed to listen to that little voice inside trying to warn me that I was walking down a bad path. I would continue to perform on the world stage desperately trying to gain my identity. Ignoring the inner sadness slowly tightening around me, I didn't realize that underneath this drive was a deep desire to just be accepted. I became a slave to my own empire, running without a purpose, and I didn't even know it.

Have you ever heard that we all have a story to tell? Do you believe it? Do you think you have a story that anyone else would really want to hear or really even care about? Relentlessly pursuing me my whole life the Lord would speak to me, but the storm inside of me and noise around me would always drown out His voice. Well, one day, somehow, I was able to hear and listen to His voice. He began to whisper to my heart to share my story. Writing not being close to anything that resembles a talent of mine, my initial reaction was, "You want me to do what?"

God was calling me to the ridiculous.

Maya Angelou captures it best when she said: "There is no greater agony than bearing an untold story inside you." I kind of liked the idea that my story was untold, but it was hard to wrap my head around the idea that the Creator of the universe seriously wanted me to write my story and share it. I tried really hard to convince Him that He had the wrong guy and that writing a book was a really bad idea, but His answer to all my excuses was always the same, **"Nevertheless, I will be with you!"** God calling people when they are not ready is a consistent theme throughout scripture and I think He does this on purpose.

OK, so back to the story…

Sooner or later, we all come to crossroads in our life where we will be given the opportunity to keep the pen and continue writing our own story or to put it down and let God write us into His story. This is a place where we will have a head-on collision with ourselves, a place where we will be forced to look into the mirror and confront ourselves to see the stuff that we are really made of. It's a place where we are faced with the piercing question: Are we having an impact on our world? Or is it having an impact on us?

This world is not our final destination—it is our journey!

His word, or what I like to call His redemptive love letter, tells us that before He shaped us in the womb He knew all about us. Did you catch that? God knew everything about us before He created us! Life has a way of blinding us to the reality that our very existence is His miracle.

We soon discover that our journey in this world has so many competing demands distracting us from our true destination that we usually miss both the journey and the destination all together. Consumed with my empire building, I lost sight of what was important in life and sadly "arriving" became more important than "becoming." Because I was so focused on what was next, I was never able to enjoy living in the moment. How much of the journey do we miss because we are so focused only on the destination? Our choices, our idols, and the stuff we covet have significant impact on us. What we fail to see is that God is more concerned with who we are becoming than with our empire building. Oddly enough, so are our wives and kids.

Power to choose; why does God allow this?

Have you ever given much thought to why God gave us the ability to make choices? Are you like me with a record breaking number of wrong choices? Have you ever thought about the impact of your choices when you barely escaped with your life on the back side of one of life's storms? I wonder if God wrestled with the idea of giving us the freedom to make choices when He created us. He may have, but He created us out of love…to love Him…and love is a choice! So the power to choose was given to us.

Journeying through life with this power to choose I would listen to every voice available to me except the voice of Truth. My misguided seeking opened the door for the enemy to come in and wreak havoc in my life. There were many things competing to become the god of my life, but unfortunately I won and I became that god. Newton's third law of motion profoundly states that for every action, there is an equal and opposite reaction. So when we ignore the truth of God's word and choose to live life our own way, for ourselves, there is an equal and opposite reaction. The corruption of this world, our self-centeredness, and the enemy of our soul rob us of the truth, which slowly drags us to our place of bondage, far from the freedom we could have. There is that unmistakable pull of human nature that always wants to draw us back toward dysfunction. This is satan's plan, and when he is given the opportunity, he will steal everything from us because it is his nature. I have allowed him to take much from me! How about you?

Jesus says in the tenth chapter of John that **"the thief comes only to steal and kill and destroy; I have come that they may have life, and have it to the full."**

Choices.

Ignoring the Lord, I became more and more blinded by my self-righteousness and foolish pride. Living life my way and making more poor choices, I eventually lost myself along the way. Sadly, I know what it feels like to stand at life's edge and not know myself anymore—to be lost in my own misery. I know how much it hurts to pretend that I don't feel life's pains anymore and how numbing it is to experience the crushing anguish of hitting rock bottom. This is the shattered reality that I chose when it was all left up to me. I was desperately lost.

The good news is that my circumstances were not hopeless, and neither is yours. By the endless magnitude of His Grace and through the power of His spirit, hope does eclipse hopelessness.

The questions before me were not easy!

King Solomon, a man who had experienced everything, challenges us with a piercing question of vivid clarity: "What does it profit us if we gain the whole world and lose our soul? My vanity of vanities chasing down the winds has left me so empty inside." This empty darkness consumes our hearts until we come to that day of hope when we allow His light to shine upon us.

My life is still messy, and I don't have it all figured out, but even though that's my reality, my hope is to be a voice through all the noise. This is my story, my testimony, His story.

We don't yet see things clearly. We're squinting in a fog, peering through a mist. But it won't be long before the weather clears and the sun shines bright! We'll see it all then, see it all as clearly as God sees us, knowing him directly just as he knows us! —1 Corinthians 13:12 (MSG)

Defeated, broken, and numbed by a quiet desperation, I hid my face in my hands, fighting to hold back the tears. It was on a curbside at a Promise Keepers event in Albany, New York, in 2004, where the Lord prearranged a divine appointment with one of the pastors in our group.

"Tell me what's going on," he said. So I began to paint for him my life canvas titled *Misery*. "To be honest," I said, "my wife wants a divorce, and I feel that God has completely abandoned me! I feel like I have failed as a husband, as a father to my kids, and as an executive in the workplace. I failed myself as someone who calls himself a Christian." With trembling lips, I looked up at him and began to weep.

I had lived behind a mask watching people labor through life's difficult circumstances with an empty compassion; never offering much grace. With a distorted myopic view of my present reality, I chose to see people going through the motions of life expecting sympathy without any hope of a new tomorrow. I had convinced myself that they followed some scripted destiny with hopeless desperation. My perspective was so distorted.

With self-righteous arrogance, I would judge people because of the reckless choices they made, always offering condemnation instead of my love. Over time, my inside reality became rooted with a deep contempt fueled at the expense of others. No one could have ever convinced me that my problems resulted from reckless choices I had made, as I silenced any criticism from others. I was about to look into the mirror and confront the real me.

I never realized that the imposter was me.

My soul was about to have a midnight.

The one who walks in the darkness does not know where he is going. —John 12:35 (ESV)

My kids would call me at work and ask me if I could come to one of their events, and I always responded with an excuse, telling them that my work was really important. I would get calls from my wife wondering if I would be home to eat dinner with the family or hoping that I wouldn't be working late again. My weekends were wasted as I spent more time in the office giving more of myself to the taskmasters. I would find more and more to do to feed on the empty acceptance which never seemed to satisfy. Business trips required me to start traveling internationally, and I would always choose to travel alone without any thought of inviting my family. I would come home from a late night at the office and selfishly choose a silent retreat right into the home office to continue my work, further isolating my wife and kids. What I didn't see was the contempt that began to take root between my wife and me. My family was slowly slipping away, and I was letting it.

Acting from a self-authored script on my own stage of life, I foolishly performed to the audience of this world, only seeing Jesus as a supplement to the playbill. I never knew the world looked at me through stained-glass eyes as it observed the apex of my achievements. I convinced everyone that my marriage was perfect, that my success in the corporate world was the greatest achievement ever, and that the material stuff and the financial success I obtained somehow made me someone. I convinced myself that I was in complete control of the world I created and that I was absolutely untouchable as long as I had my stuff to hide behind. With broad brushstrokes, I painted this far-fetched illusion that I alone was the motivating force behind all this success.

Arrogantly striving to live up to the expectations of this performance-oriented view of the world, I built a present-day tower of Babel with my own hands—stone by stone. I learned the difficult lesson that a preoccupation with "self" distorts our perspective to view everything and everyone primarily based on the way they affect us in the moment. My relationships became more and more self-serving, and success, position, and material possessions became my security and my reality. The extent of this foolishness did not leave much space for my family and God in my fractured and fragmented life. At this stage in my life, God was simply a convenience, and I hid behind the misused word *Christian* as so many of us do. James Hudson Taylor, the English missionary to China, tells it like it is, "Christ is either Lord of all, or He is not Lord at all."

Our internal and external reality must be centered in God.

With this foolish and self-centered attitude, I created a god that only met my selfish needs, and sadly enough, I was OK with that for much of my life. We have our iPods, our iPads and sadly we have our iGods. I was completely consumed by the disease of self, and it raced through my veins, eating away at my very soul like cancer.

Good understanding wins favor, but the way of the unfaithful is hard. —Proverbs 13:15 (NIV)

We grumble that living life God's way is too tough, too boring, or for some reason, we will miss out on something while we destroy ourselves walking the road of the devil.

> The natural life in each of us is something self-centered, something that wants to be petted and admired, to take advantage of other lives, to exploit the whole universe. —C. S. Lewis

If you start thinking to yourselves, "I did all this. And all by myself. I'm rich. It's all mine!"—well, think again. Remember that GOD, your God, gave you the strength to produce all this wealth so as to confirm the covenant that he promised to your ancestors—as it is today. If you forget, forget GOD, your God, and start taking up with other gods, serving and worshiping them, I'm on record right now as giving you firm warning: that will be the end of you; I mean it—destruction. You'll go to your doom—the same as the nations GOD is destroying before you; doom because you wouldn't obey the Voice of GOD, your God. —Deuteronomy 8:17–20 (MSG)

Why is it that most of us become spiritually lazy as we accept and embrace a passive existence stumbling through the shadows of life looking for love and acceptance? Have you ever noticed that we actually go out of our way to stay off the rough roads of life? It seems that our primary objectives become securing a peaceful retreat from the world, thinking only about ourselves, and finding a hiding place from the turbulence of life. We all seem to find it so much easier to simply go along with the status quo, which over time actually leads to a life of heart-numbing mediocrity, and we settle for something less than God's best.

Does God share with us in His word some thoughts about this? I think He does. Consider the story of Moses. God heard the cries of the oppressed Israelite slaves, and He enters history to deliver them from the tyranny of Pharaoh and the bondage of Egypt. After the captives have been set free from Egypt, God meets with them in the wilderness to make them His people. They enter into a covenant with God promising to love and to serve Him in response to His gracious acts of deliverance. God then promises them a land in which they could be His people.

God actually hangs out with these people wanting to connect with them in a loving relationship. Can you imagine that? That would be awesome! If that happened to us, we would be convinced! Convinced for life!

Wouldn't we?

Well, let's see what happens...

When the Israelites entered into the Promised Land, they built altars and sanctuaries to worship God and began living as His people. Years passed, they settled into the land and became way too comfortable drinking from the fountains of complacency. The passion they had once celebrated for their deliverance out of bondage slowly began to fade. Sound familiar? Many of us serve God as long as it's convenient. For many of us, this transformation unravels from Sunday to Monday.

The priests tried to maintain the sanctuaries throughout the land and to keep the worship alive, but the people could see little advantage in serving God from their places of comfort and prosperity. They became so absorbed with their own self-interests that their commitment to God faded away. In time, their hearts became divided, and they began to worship other gods. Like so many of us today, they never totally abandoned the worship of the God who brought them out of Egypt; they simply added into that worship all the other gods they wanted to serve. They gradually began to forget who they were as God's people and the new generation of children growing up had finally abandoned God for pursuit of their own pleasure. The book of Judges ends with one of the most chilling verses in the Bible: *People did whatever they felt like doing. (MSG)*

They lost perspective of God…

Does this sound vaguely familiar?

Are you getting this?

When we substitute a life with God with the deceptions and promises this world has to offer, all of our dreams will fade and the mighty walls of our storehouses will come crashing down, but we never know when.

Fractured

I thought I had it all under control, holding my fate in my own hands, but with a blind recklessness, I lost sight of God and drifted way off course. In March 2004, a cold darkness stirred on the wind and cast a deep shadow over my blue skies—a day I will never forget.

It was a Friday night, and I had just closed a major business deal that had consumed my attention for about a year. Soaring high on the adrenaline rush of this great performance, I jumped in my car and called home to see if my wife wanted me to pick something up for dinner. "Hey, I know it's late, but would you like me to stop at the sub shop and pick something up for dinner?" In a lifeless voice, she said that she didn't want anything, so I picked up a sandwich for myself. After continuing to meet my own needs, I stopped at the variety store to pick up a bottle of wine and a video so we could all celebrate my victory. Having a nice evening all planned out, I walked in the door totally ignorant of the thickening plot closing in around me.

I ran upstairs to change out of my business clothes into something more comfortable and came down stairs with the movie in one hand and bottle of wine in the other hand, preparing to pour a victory drink. I asked her if she would like a glass, and she declined, which was not her usual response. So I showed her the movie I had rented and asked her if she wanted to watch it, and she declined that too, saying, "This is not going to be a good night for a movie." As I stood there puzzled and confused, she continued. "I have something to tell you…" and she handed me a folded letter. With one last glance, she turned and walked into the other room. As I came to the word '*divorce*' written upon the letter, I fell to my knees, paralyzed as my reality became a silhouette of yesterday arriving at the edge of a broken heart. My happily-ever-after turned to dust.

Could this broken heart ever hope again?

Fade to black…

Soaring high as my sails of self-delusion become swollen by the rushing wind of my selfish pride, I had arrived home to my tower, which I thought could never be breached. With a vengeance, a storm blew in with callous ferocity and toppled its walls—my destruction. I was devastated by a letter of divorce without choice; my wife had written the final chapter of this marriage. It was over, and oneness became fractured and the sting of rejection crippling!

I was shaken by hurricane-force winds.

"I hate divorce," says the GOD of Israel. GOD-of-the-Angel-Armies says, "I hate the violent dismembering of the 'one flesh' of marriage." So watch yourselves. Don't let your guard down… — Malachi 2:16 (MSG)

It's impossible to fully understand the sorrows of divorce unless you have journeyed through its dark valleys of anguish. I have learned that these valleys only yield a desolate emptiness to anything that was once close and dear. During the agonizing process of divorce, we do not have the capacity to clearly see that we are blindly making the choice to end a marriage, a family, and are starting a vicious circle that only erodes. People have no idea of the painful realities of what lies on the other side of the violent ripping of a one-flesh covenant God intended. Divorce is always destructive, and its ripple effects are far-reaching and long-lasting. No one would argue that love and intimacy are essential to any marriage relationship, but when we assume that love and intimacy alone will sustain a marriage is when problems begin to emerge. When we build sandcastles around our hopes, dreams, and expectations, it all is violently swept away when the tidewater comes raging in. This modern culture has reduced a God-given covenant between a husband and wife into a self gratifying contract, complete with terms, conditions, indemnification and an exit clause!

As the scene unfolds at the last supper, Jesus shares with His disciples that one of them would betray Him, and the frightening part is that no one knows who it is! Jesus then goes on to establish a covenant with His disciples by the breaking of the bread and the drinking of wine, and guess who gets exposed?

Judas!

The Judas spirit always looks for intimacy without moving into a covenant relationship and has no issue with rejection and betrayal. Like many of us, we want all the benefits of a marriage relationship, but we do not want it to cost us anything; we do not want covenant. We fail to recognize the terms of surrender with our marriages and our relationship with the Lord. We do not move into a covenant relationship looking to see what we can get out of it; we look for what we can give!

After we make a marriage commitment or covenant to each other, it's critical to cleave and become united as one emotionally, physically, and spiritually. It means that together we celebrate the joys that come our way, it means that we embrace the trials and tribulations that will come our way, and it means we work together to the best of our abilities to resolve all the conflicts. Most importantly, it means that we love and accept each other.

When a marriage relationship is built on knowing that you will be there for each other, no matter what, it creates a safe place for a deep intimacy to develop forging a lasting bond that will withstand the test and trials of time. Only by building your marital foundation upon Jesus Christ can you hope to achieve the true intimacy that God intended for marriage. He becomes the cornerstone of the marriage! I am not saying that the breakdown of my marriage was completely my fault, but what I am saying is that I am accountable for my contribution. Maintaining innocence in a divorce would fool no one. I'm not suggesting that this is an absolute for every situation, but it usually takes two, and the reality is that the story is rarely simple.

As the illusions of this worldview spin around me out of time and frame, the walls of my tower of Babel crumble and fall! One could almost hear the demonic laughter and cheers coming from the darkness of the abyss as each stone smashes to the ground like hardened drops of rain.

> It is always night when a man goes from Christ to follow his own purposes. It is always night when a man listens to the call of evil rather than the summons of good. It is always night when hate puts out the light of love. It is always night when a person turns his back on Jesus. —William Barclay

"We have to tell the kids," she said.

I stood at the front of our house, looking through the glass and watching a scene in slow motion. The school bus stopped, and I watched my children run up the driveway without a care in the world. My heart sank, and I became numb, knowing that these words would completely shatter the only secure world they had ever known. The piercing message was delivered to our daughter, which was a devastating blow to this once joy-filled little girl as tears of sorrow streamed down her precious little cheeks; a scene that will be etched within my mind forever. The message was next delivered to our son, who was too young at the time to understand, but I know that something changed in him.

That day I saw the tears. I heard the tears…I felt the tears!

Our marriage was fractured, our kids were fractured, and my heart was fractured.

I didn't want to live without them, and I didn't want to say good-bye.

A moment in time had passed before my eyes!

Alone

Asked to leave the familiar security of my house, I would cry myself to sleep in a sleeping bag on the hard basement floor of my friend's house. With my fragile, battered soul and any remaining hope ripped from me, I would simply collapse from the weight of my life. Images pounded me like the relentless, battering waves against a rocky sea shore as I replayed events in my mind. Chaos entered my life as my entire world eroded and washed away all around me. I became so completely crushed and broken that a part of me wanted to die because I couldn't stand the torment of this deep, gut-wrenching pain. Broken and alone, I would silently drown within a puddle of my tears fading into this scene of sorrow.

My spirit ached!

> The greatest blessing spiritually is the knowledge that we are destitute; until we get there Our Lord is powerless. —Oswald Chambers

I found myself standing between fear of the unknown and the weight of my circumstances bearing down on me, which felt like the death of any remaining hope. The Israelites found themselves in such a place. They could see the expanse of dry land the Red Sea had once occupied; the mighty walls of water supernaturally held back by the awesome hand of God; and they could see that the armies of Egypt were bearing down on them. In addition to their not clearly seeing the other shore of the parted Red Sea and perhaps their apprehension that the walls of water could come crashing down on them was their fear of the unknown, and the Egyptian army was the means of their certain death. They became paralyzed by fear.

The emptiness is now very real!

These familiar shadows are closing in!

A suffocating fear descends upon me!

There is nowhere left to hide!

I feel so alone!

My heart was broken, and I had journeyed to a place where I'd convinced myself that I had made too many mistakes to come home. I felt like an autumn leaf spiraling out of control, falling to the ground waiting to be soon forgotten under winter's snow. I would ask God over and over again when the pain would be over and what the purpose was for all of this.

Lying here in the midnight of my anguish…

This midnight goes on as I fade away…

How could this happen to me?

It hurts!

Worn out from the contact sport of life, I began to lose my will to fight. Losing my faith and wondering what I believed, I knelt at my bedside and begin to pour out my heart to the Lord, soaking my pillow with my tears. My heart exploded as waves of emotions crushed me. With not much left to steal my attention away, I finally allowed Jesus to walk to me. He found me in my hiding place.

"Are You there, God? It's me…I hope You remember me…I have nothing left—I am a lifeless, empty soul of a man who is afraid, alone, and worn out from life. I'm paralyzed by the thought of morning, as a new day will only drag me further into reaping what I've sown. God, I am so, so sorry! Please find a place in Your heart for me, to forgive me for the things I've done…It's not what I wanted to do. I need to hear Your voice tonight…to know that You are here. Living with this shame and guilt is crushing me. These empty feelings are consuming my thoughts like pounding waves! I want to feel something! I have made a mess of things and I don't know what to do God, I need You! I long for Your embrace! I can't find my way out! I've tried just about everything to dull the pain of this life I have made. I'm hurting so much and I desperately need You! Take me far away from this broken place! I don't want to stay here another day! I want to feel something real. Please God, please…bring me back to Your forgiveness and grace! I don't know what else to pray."

Sometimes we need the pain of our circumstances to get us un-stuck from our place of misery and to move us toward a place of health, a place of freedom, and a place of change.

"Lord, I tried so hard!"

"Take me away to the place where my heart can sing again!"

Once my misery became greater than my fear, I was able to risk running out to face my fear of the unknown. It was the anguishing pain of my circumstances, a failed marriage, and a fractured family, that moved me to want to change. In a way, I needed the Egyptian army to come at me to challenge my fear. Sometimes God allows us to fall into these places for the purpose of moving us forward. I did not conquer all my fears at this point, but I got unstuck and could begin to walk out of my fear of the unknown.

Expose these empty lies!

Replace this fear I have inside!

I have nowhere to run!

Through choices that I have made over the years, I lost my way home; I was looking to myself and searching for nothing. Standing paralyzed in this frightening night, my scene of hope seemed so distant, imprisoned within the dark, cold chamber I had retreated to from life.

I couldn't find my way out.

Desperately praying and hoping for a new tomorrow, I wrote these words from within the shadows of my circumstances:

Divine Oneness

In an instant my body was cast into a raging storm, with unimaginable intensity, too much for me to endure.

I fell hard into the cruel, icy-cold waters of this dark unrelenting torment, crushed by the unforgiving waves as this reality began to pierce my entire existence.

I wanted so much to cry out to be spared the intense pain of this terrifying nightmare; I began to descend into the deep emptiness of hurt, loneliness, and absolute hopelessness.

The baggage that I have been burdening myself with over the years began to pull me ever so deeper into this darkness.

Completely shattered and my entire world crumbling away; I fade, thinking that death would be easier. I am smashed into the hard bottom of this anguish.

I cry out to my Lord with absolute lament, completely broken and my spirit crushed! My will is gone, I cannot do this! I surrender! Into Your arms I fall! I yield full control of my life to You!

Please God, please renew in me a new heart, change me…save me! Shattering the bitter cold darkness, a blinding warm light appeared before me.

With outstretched hands my Lord in all of His glory stood before me. He placed His gentle hand on my shoulder and said to me, "I loved you so much that I died for you. I want so much to be a part of your life."

Little by little, He slowly brought me to my feet as I cried tears of joy and then gracefully wrapped His comforting arms around me and said, "You have been gone for a long time. I missed you so much; come find your rest!"

Like a miracle, all the corrupt baggage that burdened me was instantly taken from me by my Lord, and a warm gentle covering of peace enveloped my broken body and my spirit began to heal.

The Lord lifted me up and carried me out of the unremitting storm onto a tranquil shoreline which was sheltered by a vast impenetrable angelic host.

The storm even now rages around me, but I begin to stop being consumed by the waves and began to affix my stare to my Lord Jesus;
I take refuge in Him. My Lord said this to me with authority, "Truth, unconditional love, full obedience to My word…do My will!

With this I will give you the strength to persevere! All things are possible for those who truly love Me."

I then asked my Lord, "Lord, why did I fail? Is there hope? How can healing begin?" He answered and said, "Without My love in your life you are unable to understand divine oneness! The becoming of one flesh! To love her like I love the church!"

Completely consumed by this shattering sorrow, I slipped further into the shadows of brokenness and hopelessness. Lifeless and alone on my friend's cold basement floor, I curled up in my sleeping bag, retreated within the silent prison walls of my mind, and arrived at the end of human existence. I was angry at my former wife, angry at life, angry at God, angry at everything. In so much pain and sinking deeper into the anguish of this hell, I was held captive by every thought that took into this bitterness consuming me.

The question of "Why?" began to haunt my every thought.

Arriving at a crucial crossroad in my life, forced to reflect, I was ready to see that my wife had tried to reach out to me and share her hurt. My sister had tried to get through to me; others in my family and those close to me had even tried. None of the signals made it through the barriers I built to protect myself from my past hurts. None of the signs penetrated my pride.

I had been unreachable.

There are so many empty reasons for this past I created, where excuses just don't hold anymore. I have been stricken with this "self" affliction; these foolish decisions were all my own, and I never saw the warning signs to save me from myself. Never seeing the consequences of my choices, the floodwaters of despair beginning to rise above my head, I was drowning in an ocean of tears! Wondering if I could ever escape from this place I've made.

From inside the belly of the fish Jonah prayed: *"In my distress I called to the LORD, and he answered me. From the depths of the grave I called for help, and you listened to my cry." (Jonah 2:1–2 [NIV])*. Jonah chose a course of action that was selfish. He completely ignored God and ran from Him after receiving a word asking him to travel to Nineveh to preach to them. Furthermore, on his journey to escape his destiny, he knowingly endangered the lives of others on the ship where he was hiding. What is truly awesome is that God heard his cry and delivered him even amid his stupidity.

The harsh reality is that when we live our lives on our own terms and pursue a life separate from God, we are in rebellion. The good news is that if you find yourself in this place; know that the Lord wants to redeem you because He loves you! Things won't be easy. You will most likely have to walk through the pain and not around it. You will still experience hardships, but coming back to the Lord opens the door to redemption and deliverance. He will walk with you. He will hold you. He is safe!

Hardship

Stephen, full of the Spirit of God, began preaching to the people and ended his divinely inspired message with the following,

And you continue, so bullheaded! Calluses on your hearts, flaps on your ears! Deliberately ignoring the Holy Spirit, you're just like your ancestors. Was there ever a prophet who didn't get the same treatment? Your ancestors killed anyone who dared talk about the coming of the Just One. And you've kept up the family tradition—traitors and murderers, all of you. You had God's Law handed to you by angels—gift-wrapped!—and you squandered it! —Acts 7:51–53 (MSG)

At that point, the wild and rioting crowd had heard enough, dragged Stephen out of town, and stoned him to death. As the rocks continued to smash hard against Stephen, with each life-draining blow, he asked Jesus to forgive the crowd. One of the spectators at this event was a young man named Saul, who stood by congratulating the murderers.

Let's take a moment to review the impressive credentials of Saul, which were viewed in high esteem back in biblical times. He had a legitimate birth, being circumcised on the eight day; he was an Israelite from the elite tribe of Benjamin; he had a strict and devout adherent to God's law; he was a defender of the purity of his religion, even to the point of persecuting Christians; and he was a meticulous observer of the scriptures…but he was living a life in complete opposition to God.

Saul's life plan was built on pretense. What seems so right to us becomes a fatal trap, but God loves us too much to leave us where we're at. What Saul didn't realize is that the road to Damascus would put him on a collision course with God and that on the other side of this redemptive confrontation he would be given a new name. Saul becomes Paul.

A confrontation to expose who he really was!

A confrontation that knocked him off his horse!

One day, it's all going fine and the next day, the bottom drops out with no real explanation. It only takes a split second for everything to change. Maybe you lost your job, or a family member had a serious accident…fill in your own personal hardship. Whether or not you are presently encountering hardship in your life, you can be certain that they will come as we live in a fallen and broken world. You can't escape life without hurt. Jesus even said,

I've told you all this so that trusting me, you will be unshakable and assured, deeply at peace. In this godless world you will continue to experience difficulties. But take heart! I've conquered the world. — John 16:33 (MSG)

The second chapter of Corinthians provides a glimpse into the hardship Paul had to endure and walk through. Five times he received the forty lashes minus one. Three times he was beaten with rods; he was stoned; three times he was shipwrecked; he spent a night and a day in the open sea; and he was constantly on the move. He had been in danger from rivers; from bandits from his own countrymen, in the city, in the country, and at sea; and from false brothers. He had labored and toiled and had often gone without sleep; he had known hunger and thirst and had often gone without food; he had also experienced coldness and nakedness.

The very credentials that once defined his place of security and identity were dumped in exchange for Jesus. Paul made a choice with life's hardships…he gloried in them. He came to a place in his relationship with God where God became everything good and true in his life. He began to see that God shaped his character through these hardships.

When we experience hardships in life, we can let them destroy us or we can allow the Lord to walk with us through them, letting Him shape and refine us along the way. Most of us get extremely angry with God and blame Him when hard times come and we lose the opportunity to get closer to Him and miss out on what He may be trying to teach us. God understands the human heart, and He understands that for us to become all that He hopes for us, there will be seasons of hardship.

Hardships.

They will come, but how we react to them is entirely up to us. They can overwhelm as questions invade our hearts and minds. They test our perseverance because we cannot see a light at the end of a very dark tunnel. We find ourselves in situations where darkness deepens and we do not know where to turn. We can be confident that He will either cause our hardships to cease or carry us through them. In His strength we will survive. May we run to the Lord in the midst of our hardships so that we will grow nearer to Him as we learn to trust Him! Not easy.

The crucible for silver and the furnace for gold, but the Lord tests the heart. —*Proverbs 17:3 (NIV)*

> But before we choose to follow God's will, a crisis must develop in our lives. This happens because we tend to be unresponsive to God's gentler nudges. He brings us to the place where He asks us to be our utmost for Him and we begin to debate. He then providentially produces a crisis where we have to decide—for or against. That moment becomes a great crossroads in our lives. If a crisis has come to you on any front, surrender your will to Jesus absolutely and irrevocably. —Oswald Chambers

This time in my life was hard, but I began to slowly move in a better direction as I developed an unquenchable desire to find answers and to better understand God. Through these hardships, I am learning that He will give us the grace we need to get through them and that He is able to accomplish what He wants for our lives if we let Him. I still had the wrong perspective, that all of this was somehow His fault, and I was still angry with God, but through it all, God continued to sustain me in His grace while I sorted it all out. I once heard it said that the amazing thing about God is that He knows us and loves us anyway. God is confident to bring about all the changes that are needed in our lives. All He needs is a willing heart.

Isn't He an awesome God?

I was open to the whole idea of this "Jesus thing" back in junior high and decided to let Him step into my life, not really understanding the part about first losing my life. As Jesus stood there knocking on the door of my heart, I had let Him in, but only as a guest. I had never turned the key to my heart over to Him completely. No one truly explained to me that when you abandon your life for Christ, you find it. I had jumped at the idea of heaven, eternal life, and salvation, but I hadn't grasped that what God really wanted was my heart—He wanted me. He didn't want my stuff; He didn't want my achievements; He didn't care about my title…He just wanted a relationship with me; to know me, to embrace me and to love me. I could talk all day about how much I loved God, but those were empty words with little action. So for much of my life, I lived juxtaposed between the places of knowing the truth of God's word, always choosing to place my selfish desires above His—seeking only to satisfy my own selfish pleasures, completely self-absorbed with all the many idols I pursued and worshipped.

Those who cling to worthless idols forfeit the grace that could be theirs. —Jonah 2:8 (NIV)

What a treacherous place to live.

I spent much of my life living for me, looking for love in false idols, obtaining wealth and stuff, and spending all my energy trying to protect it all, and in the process, I had been losing my life and falling deeper into bondage! There was an undercurrent of fear that drove my desire to accumulate stuff. My satisfaction was in what I had, how it was stored and my own capacity to take care of my life. I wanted to be a good husband and father as these roles were important to me, but I had blindly assumed that I could sustain a healthy family dynamic by giving them my leftovers from the pursuit of these things. I completely missed the joy of a relationship with the Lord, and the sad part is that I had it all in front of me and available to me in Jesus…I simply missed it! Like Pontius Pilate, I was arm's length from the best opportunity of my life!

I journeyed through life with a big emptiness, a big hole right in the center of my heart. I didn't know what it was; I only knew that I had a serious love deficit and it needed to be filled with something—with anything. Blinded by the hurts and pain of my past, I easily found ways of filling this hole with counterfeit affections; things that looked so good up front, things that this world told me I needed, things that I became a prisoner to and was ultimately destroyed by. Behind these strongholds of delusion and deception, I learned to fill this hole with an insatiable desire for wealth, power, control, and success. Stained by ignorance, wrong choices, and complete blindness, I found myself in a situation of mocking God for many years and making the world my taskmaster! This is essentially direct disobedience concealed behind the mask of self-deception.

I thought I knew the Lord during this pursuit to fill my void, but I was actually pushing Him, the one thing that could actually fill it, further and further away. I could not find a way to escape the mirrors in my mind that continued to feed me all these lies. The lies became the truth.

I became so blind, and I found it so easy to move to the rhythm of this world that I believed the lies and illusions of its promises. The world promised me everything I thought I needed; only I found that these promises took everything from me leaving me completely empty at my core—my soul was bankrupt. A single heart becomes divided; I gave my heart to these pleasures, and she gave her heart to another. There was a sobering symmetry between us, because we had both looked for affirmation outside of the marriage. Although I chose a source of affirmation such as work that could be considered biblically and socially acceptable, in God's eyes, the principle of the problem was the same. This American dream becomes our American tragedy.

> "You cannot cooperate with Jesus in becoming what He wants you to become and simultaneously be what the world desires to make you. If you would say, "Take the world but give me Jesus," then you must deny yourself and take up your cross. The simple truth is that your "self" must be put to death in order for you to get to the point where for you to live is Christ. What will it be? The world and you, or Jesus and you? You do have a choice to make." —Kay Arthur

Why is it so difficult for us to see His awesome grace?

Why is it so difficult for us to see His love?

Why don't we run into His arms of mercy and forgiveness?

He offers these and so much more as gifts! Freely!

There is an incredible, deep intimacy that we can have with our Heavenly Father that is indescribable, but we somehow convince ourselves that He is holding out on us or that there is something better, and we conform to the darkness and patterns of this lost and broken world. We become tangled up in all our own cares, which becomes such a lonely affair; we close our eyes and let everything good and true pass by; and we become more and more numb. We seem to always stumble on this journey of life because we continue to consume endless head knowledge and feed off the wisdom of this world. Most of us actually hide behind bitterness and hatred to numb our painful sorrows.

Why do we do this?

Our head knowledge creates an enormous, empty void. It only becomes real when it moves from our heads to our hearts and we action it out in life. I had the truth as just information; I didn't have it as context or content or relationship. You know that on this side of the cross, under the new covenant, we have more insight and knowledge than those under the old covenant, and even to this extent, we act the same because we do nothing with this knowledge. The gospel message must sink deep within our heart, saturate our being, and show up in our actions before we can effectively help others understand and apply it in their lives. We can't give away that which we do not have or are not capable of. Take a lake, for example; for a lake to be filled, it needs a river to bring it fresh water (meeting our needs), but once the lake is filled, it needs an outlet for the overflow, which is meeting others' needs (selflessness).

A lake without an inlet dries up, and a lake without an outlet becomes a swamp!

Experience has taught me that it is impossible to feel the heartbeat of the Lord when all of this stuff is stuck in our heads. We need to humble ourselves, come before the Lord with a spirit of repentance, and ask Him to take our hearts and resuscitate them.

Finding ourselves within the living pages of God's word, it becomes clear that our dreams fade into the night as our lives are interrupted and we lose complete control of our own circumstances. We are thrown overboard into the stormy seas of uncertainty without a lifeline, as Jonah was, and for the first time in our lives, our nature to control is ripped from our hands, and we are forced to depend completely on God. In the book of Hosea, it says that God will lure us out into the desert and speak tenderly to us and will make the Valley of Achor, which literally means "trouble," a door of hope.

Many life events, choices, and circumstances defined the strongholds I had erected to conceal this inner pain, hurt, and brokenness over time became fused with the core fabric of my existence. At least I had convinced myself of this. I found myself living through a cruel lesson in creative suffering, and I became the victim of these experiences of serious deprivation and shame, stained with a coat of abandonment and rejection. As I reflect on the past that I had anchored myself to, I so longed for that which I thought would never be gained—the love and acceptance of the Father.

Wounds

A mysterious silence gripped the air that cold January morning in 1969, as the day of anticipation had finally arrived. This destiny moment begins in the sterile sanctuary of a hospital room with medical equipment filling the white space while soothing lullaby sounds captivated those waiting as if in a daydream. The sounds were mixed with a permeating hospital antiseptic smell that causes most to enter a state of numbness.

Something begins to happen, mysteriously breaking the lucidity of the room as everyone wakens from his or her slumber, revealing facial expressions of apprehension and anticipation. The innocence of creation is about to invade this hospital room as I begin to open my eyes within the darkness. My little heart begins to beat with an anxious rhythm as I hear the chaotic voices calling my name from a distant place, far beyond the peace and comfort of this womb, the only place that I have ever known before Heaven's embrace.

The mystery of birth begins to move me from my place of peace, from my place of comfort. The voices become louder and clearer as a bright white light explodes into view, invading my hiding place. Not understanding what was happening to me, I panic, which causes me to turn my little body, creating a breach delivery.

Events begin to assault the stillness of my hiding place.

Confusion and fear surround me.

My hiding place of peace and comfort fades to black as chaos rushes in like a flood forever changing my existence. The doctors, fighting against time, attempt to change the position of my little body for delivery, but my mother is jolted and jumps, which sends me tumbling in the womb, and my leg goes numb. Losing the inner battle to hold back my tears, I cry out into the silence of the womb because this paralyzing pain pierces me deeply. Fighting for my life now, I hold on, trying to stay away from the light as it has already caused me so much pain. I cry out with a silent anguish, "Leave me alone!" as something deep within my soul presses hard against my will as I fight to simply exist.

My falling…

My screaming…

My crying…

The doctors wrestle with this mysterious struggle as I continue to fight to be born. Tired, scared, and wishing this nightmare to end, I give up and let go with a silent emptiness to live as I am delivered into the cold winter of this new world on the other side of comfort. With an unwelcoming velocity, I am born into a frightening world of tears; my peace is shattered by the confusion of the unknown.

Broken like a mirror smashed to pieces!

Hearing the deafening whispers mixed with expressions of joy and concern, the doctors and my family look upon me. I struggle with the reality of this birth as my mother holds me to comfort my pain. The light of this new world reveals the painful gift of imperfection; my little leg is fractured!

The doctors worked attentively to repair my fractured leg without understanding that this gift was not to be embraced in the physical, but a foreshadowing, a symbol of the curse of anguished brokenness I would endure within this life. My birthmark became a self-fulfilling prophecy as life continued the process of wounding me and breaking me.

As we journey through the mystery of life our circumstances confront us with the reality that brokenness is difficult to avoid in the world we live in. This symbol of my birth will forever remind me of the fight to simply exist—a symbol that was never intended for this precious little spirit.

Eden fades into the night as a distant memory.

There is only pain!

There is only fear!

There are only tears!

Paradise has become my place to cry.

This world is not my home.

Before I shaped you in the womb, I knew all about you. Before you saw the light of day, I had holy plans for you. —Jeremiah 1:5a (MSG)

This symbol of my birth would not be healed when the cast was removed; the scars of these wounds to come would define the person that I would become. The pain of birth, the turbulence of life, and the noise of desperate circumstances continued to drown out the soft, still, gentle voice of the Lord. Heaven's embrace calls out to me…

"My precious child, I know everything about you! Out of My deep love, I sculpted you from nothing into something beautiful as I formed you in your mother's womb. All the days of your life have I prepared for you—before you took your first breath. I promised you that I will always be with you and I will never abandon you. You will continue to face difficulties in this world, but take heart for I have conquered the world! If you let Me, I will show up and take care of you and bring you back home to Me. I am God and I know what I'm doing! I have it all planned out—plans to take care of you, not abandon you, plans to give you the future you hope for. Lift all the broken pieces of your life

to Me! If you only knew, how much you mean to Me, if you only knew how much I love you…if you only knew!"

Cry

This lost, hurt "little boy" inside this hardened, calloused shell of a man would weep with an intense sorrow almost every day as empty, silent tears, hidden so deep within the dark chambers of relentless anguish, would go unheard. What this "little boy" so longed and hoped for was the precious gift, the affirmation of the Father, the healing words that would remove the deep scars of brokenness: "This is my beloved son, in whom I am well pleased." With such acceptance so void in my life, this respect-starved man of emptiness simply concluded that more work, greater accumulation of symbols of success and worldly praise would finally give me the strength to come out of my hiding place and hear the life-healing words.

Hearing the deafening whispers of voices mixed with expressions of joy and concern, the doctors and my family look upon me. I struggle with the reality of this birth as my mother holds me to comfort my pain. The light of this new world reveals the painful gift of imperfection; my little leg is fractured! The doctors worked attentively to repair my fractured leg without understanding that this gift was not to be embraced in the physical but was a foreshadowing, a symbol of the curse of anguished brokenness I would endure within this life. My birthmark became a self-fulfilling prophecy as life continued the process of wounding me and breaking me.

Pressing ever so hard against this diminishing hope of gaining acceptance and approval, I convinced myself that this purpose was unattainable and my hopes and dreams shatter in the many tears I cry! I arrived at the point in my life where this emptiness and brokenness actually becomes my symbolic birthright represented by my broken leg. I would struggle to fully walk in this life. It's no wonder I developed an unquenchable appetite for applause, wealth, and power from any source in an attempt to compensate for the loss, to fill this void.

With my broken leg, I would limp through life.

This blurred reality defined my focus outwardly, a public pursuit which left my inner world empty. Behind this intense quest for power was a deep desire for love. As I soon learned, my heart was lifeless, without a beat, and my soul was sick.

I slipped slowly into a shrouded pit as the sorrows and hurt of the scarring wounds from within tore me down. Listening to the faint voices masquerading through the mist and haze of discouragement as the answer to these chains that have entangled me, I slowly leave behind the will to hold on and let go. The core issue we all face is when the self becomes our god and we worship it. When the self is our god, we strive to make all of life revolve around it, and with a consuming zeal, we seek to satisfy empty vanity.

I finally came to the end of myself.

So hurt and wounded, I worshiped at the altar of pride, began living this life for only myself, and walked blindly down this wide path, foolishly reaching out for the things that kept destroying me. Envying the lives and ambitions of others and swimming in the seas of sensuality that fueled this selfishness, I somehow believed that they would all have what I needed! It was cold within this dark reality as the wind blew intensely against my face, stumbling through the shadow over and over. It's not supposed to be this way.

In Proverbs 13, verse 12a, the writer tells us "hope deferred makes the heart sick." I had arrived at a place in my life where life became discouraging and hopeless. I had lost all hope, and it made me sick. Being at this place is a scary proposition, and it brings you to the edge of despair.

I ran so far from home desperately looking for a hope made of stone.

Running from these memories, yearning to be held, is the cry of the son.

We need to remember that every step away from the Lord is a step in the wrong direction. When we are hurting or have failed, that is not the time to run away from the Lord. That is the time we need to run to Him!

Rise

Seeing that the once high and mighty protecting walls of Jerusalem were in absolute rubble, God decided to have a little chat with Nehemiah to rise up and rebuild them. Through divine providence, the king gave Nehemiah the authorization to return to Jerusalem to go about the business of rebuilding the walls. The process of rebuilding the walls took time, commitment, sacrifice and was met with many challenges and opposition. Make no mistake, whenever God's people say, "Let's rise up and build," satan and his goons are going to say, "Let's rise up and tear down."

Seeing that I allowed the once mighty protecting walls of my life and my heart become rubble, He wanted to do what I thought was impossible—rebuild my ruined walls. This is where I would find the strength to carry on, to stand, to rise up. It's important to know that He has already finished strong and He knows how the story is going to end! Praise God!

> "Many Christians have bought into the lie that we are worthy of God's love only when our lives are going well. If our families are happy or our jobs are meaningful, life is a success. Yet when life begins to fall apart and embarrassing sins threaten to reveal our less-than-perfect identity, we scramble to keep up a good front to present to the world—and to God. We cower and hide until we can rearrange the mask of perfection and look good again. Sadly, it is then that we wonder why we lack intimate relationships and a passionate faith. All this time, though, God is calling us to take our masks off and come openly to Him. God longs for us to know in the depths of our beings that He loves us and accepts us as we are. When we are our true selves, we can finally claim our identity as God's children and experience His pure pleasure in who we are."[i]

A "wall" is a solid structure that defines and sometimes protects an area and there are basically three types of walls: building walls, retaining walls, and exterior boundary walls.[ii] Boundary walls delineate boundaries and are used to protect areas like cities, such as the walls that once protected Jerusalem. Some of these walls are stronger than others are, but they all need upkeep and maintenance. When the apathetic distractions of the city erode further into a self-centered, empty ambition, the walls fade into the distance and become seriously neglected leaving its patiently waiting enemies free to come in.

Like a city whose walls are broken down is a man who lacks self-control. —Proverbs 25:28 (NIV)

In the process of protecting myself from further pain and brokenness, I shut out the world, everyone around me, and even God. I continued to retreat further and deeper within myself, neglecting the necessary upkeep of the very walls that God once built around me for protection. It was only a matter of time before my enemies breached the aging and crumbling walls around my life and my heart.

My choices became my prison and left me in ruins.

Unfortunately, it wasn't until I allowed the protective walls of God around me to crumble and fall to ruins that I came to a place in my life where I would allow the Lord to come back in to begin the restoration process. The enemies—the lies of the world, the corrupt nature of my self-centered flesh and the enemy of my soul—were just relentlessly beating me down. All the pain, rejection, hurt, and brokenness had to be redeemed, and only God could do this, so I had to let the rebuilding process happen no matter the cost. It's only when we humble ourselves and pray and seek His face and turn from our wicked ways that God will hear us, forgive our sins, and restore our land. The Lord will restore and redeem the brokenness in our lives if we let Him and with the rebuilding process of His walls around our lives, our hearts will again be erected to their former strength. He becomes our Strong Tower.

Whoever has no rule over his own spirit is like a city broken down, without walls. —Proverbs 25:28 (NKJV)

I have found that there is an inverse reality that I have been living that can be discovered in the Bible: God views brokenness as strength. The whole concept of recognizing brokenness as strength is so foreign to us and totally against what this world tells us.

How can brokenness be strength?

It doesn't make sense!

...and then he told me, My grace is enough; it's all you need. My strength comes into its own in your weakness. Once I heard that, I was glad to let it happen. I quit focusing on the handicap and began appreciating the gift. It was a case of Christ's strength moving in on my weakness. Now I take limitations in stride, and with good cheer, these limitations that cut me down to size--abuse, accidents, opposition, bad breaks. I just let Christ take over! And so the weaker I get, the stronger I become.—2 Corinthians 12:9, 10 (MSG)

Check this list of people out; Paul had to be broken, Moses had to be broken, Peter had to be broken, Jacob had to be broken, David had to be broken and I too, had to be broken. When we come to a place of complete brokenness, the blindness is removed from our eyes, and we see with more clarity that we can do nothing in our own strength. When this new supernatural strength through brokenness emerges within us, it is something that God can use in mighty ways.

And what he gives in love is far better than anything else you'll find. It's common knowledge that God goes against the willful proud; God gives grace to the willing humble. —James 4:6 (MSG)

As hard as this may seem, try not to fear the brokenness in your life; acknowledge it. We convince ourselves that it's easier to ignore the pain and pretend like we are OK, and we just deal with it by pushing it further down. God's desire for us is that we would bring our brokenness to Him. He longs to heal our brokenness. He is waiting for you to acknowledge it. Bring it to Him.

I couldn't ignore it anymore.

It was time for me to acknowledge it.

Heaven's embrace calls out to me…

"As I walk in the cool of the morning, I think of you, My precious child. Wondering where you are and why you have run so far from Me. It's breaking My heart. Beloved, I love you more than you can ever imagine and I miss you so much! If you only knew that all that I have and all that I am is yours to find, but you hide from me and seek the things of this world, convincing yourself that you are free. Come home to Me and I will show how to live and I will truly set you free. I love you so much! Please come back home to Me my precious child. I dream of the day when I see you running back to Me and when I can embrace you again. My child, if you only knew…"

In His presence, all of our fears are washed away! Just, remember what happened to the armies of Egypt as they pursued the Israelites: they were washed away!

You will be held by Grace!

Just let go and belong to Him!

SECOND STONE ʃ MOUNTAINS

When Elijah saw how things were, he ran for dear life to Beersheba, far in the south of Judah. He left his young servant there and then went on into the desert another day's journey. He came to a lone broom bush and collapsed in its shade, wanting in the worst way to be done with it all—to just die: "Enough of this, GOD! Take my life—I'm ready to join my ancestors in the grave!" Exhausted, he fell asleep under the lone broom bush. Suddenly an angel shook him awake and said, "Get up and eat!" He looked around and, to his surprise, right by his head were a loaf of bread baked on some coals and a jug of water. He ate the meal and went back to sleep. The angel of GOD came back, shook him awake again, and said, "Get up and eat some more—you've got a long journey ahead of you." He got up, ate and drank his fill, and set out. Nourished by that meal, he walked forty days and nights, all the way to the mountain of God, to Horeb.
1 Kings 19:3-8 (MSG)

If God be God over us, we must yield Him universal obedience in all things. He must not be over us in one thing, and under us in another, but He must be over us in everything. —Peter Bulkeley

Clarity

Out of my brokenness, I realized that it was time to let God step into the ruins of my life. Personally, I thought it would be awesome to have some of that supernatural strength, so I said to the Lord, "Go for it!" So I slowly started to let God have His way, but it didn't take long before I became impatient with the process and tried to wrestle some control back. Taking inventory of my current state of affairs, I hit the pause button and thought to myself, "Wait a second!" I had lost my hope, my family, my house, many friends, my financial resources, and almost my job, and I kept crucifying myself with the regrets of my past and the fear of my future. Furthermore, I had lived in a basement, in a dreadfully hot and small apartment, and now found my existence within a single room in a friend's home with the remainder of my stuff. I just wasn't feeling the supernatural strength, so I got on my knees and began to have a chat with the Lord, during which I basically asked Him why this was all happening, and He simply replied, **"Because I love you!"** I have to be completely honest and transparent with you: I was wondering if He could love me a little less, because this was not fun!

I could not see the picture that God was painting.

Well, I had had enough and determined that it would be best for me to use some of my own strength, and I decided to go on a hike. I really needed to clear my thoughts and getting up on top of the mountains usually was a great remedy. What I didn't realize is that God was smiling a bit because He had planned this. He had known about my circumstances from the very beginning.

Still alone, or so I thought, I concluded to head up to Mt. Lafayette in Franconia Notch, New Hampshire, and hike to the top by myself, which goes against the rule of hiking: never hike alone. My friend found out what I was about to do, and said, "Tim, you won't be alone on this hike…I am going with you."

Did you know that Elijah and Moses found themselves on just such a hike? Moses decided to take matters into his own hands with his own plan to set the Israelites free by killing an Egyptian: great plan! Elijah, after demonstrating an incredible act of God's power by calling down fire upon an altar in an awesome power play against Jezebel and the evil prophets of baal, found himself physically and emotionally exhausted to the point where he actually had had enough and asked God to take his life. I was getting close to this! Have you ever been at the water's edge with the entire Egyptian army barreling down on you? Sound familiar?

Did you realize that both Moses and Elijah were led to the same location some 500 years apart? They were both led to Mount Horeb, the mountain of God, which, translated, means "desolation." For Moses, it was forty years in the wilderness; for Elijah, it was forty days without food as he became tired of standing alone for God; and for me, it was a lifetime of living for myself. In reality, I would soon learn that it was a place of renewal, a place of new beginnings, and a place of a personal encounter with the living God: a symbolic place of intimacy where God meets us!

It was during this place of desolation, my journey to His Mountain that the Lord spoke to my heart with a resounding clarity; **"Truth, love, obedience, and do My will!"** This refreshing revelation would become the very foundation stones for the path that He was preparing before me, the path that I had to walk.

We felt like we'd been sent to death row that it was all over for us. As it turned out, it was the best thing that could have happened. Instead of trusting in our own strength or wits to get out of it, we were forced to trust God totally—not a bad idea since he's the God who raises the dead! And he did it, rescued us from certain doom. And he'll do it again, rescuing us as many times as we need rescuing. —2 Corinthians 1:9, 10 (MSG)

As I began to slowly release my grip of the fear rooted in my brokenness, the soft gentle wind of His Spirit began to prepare me for my exodus out of the Egypt I had created in my life. This journey would be brushed with plagues, an angry Pharaoh, many times of doubting God and overwhelming obstacles to overcome. Remember, it didn't take much time for God to get the Israelites out of Egypt, but it took years to get Egypt out of the Israelites. I was no different.

Many of us begin this journey from bondage to freedom only to walk so far with the Lord. We then become intoxicated with the sweet wine of complacency and again buy into the continued false promises of this world. We come to a place where

Egypt looks so good in the rearview mirror, even though it was our place of bondage, and we begin to complain. One can almost see the Lord rolling His eyes and shaking His head, saying, **"If you only knew."** This is a very dangerous place to get to and many of us sadly arrive here. It is a place where satan prowls around like a lion searching for those he can devour, lurking and looking for any area of weakness in us that has not gone to the cross so that he can use it at a strategic time. The enemy waits patiently for us to get to this place, so he can strike—and he is usually successful in taking us down. This is a place where satan will call your bluff.

Keep a cool head. Stay alert. The Devil is poised to pounce, and would like nothing better than to catch you napping. Keep your guard up. You're not the only ones plunged into these hard times. It's the same with Christians all over the world. So keep a firm grip on the faith. —1 Peter 5:8, 9 (MSG)

I was truly hoping for a short, easy sprint as so many of us do, but this race I had to run began at the base of a mountain, the mountain of God. He had brought me here to this place of new beginnings to have my mountaintop experience, to show me the way home to the Promised Land.

I know what I'm doing. I have it all planned out--plans to take care of you, not abandon you, plans to give you the future you hope for. —Jeremiah 29:11 (MSG)

I still could not see the beautiful picture He was painting, but when He brought me to the mountaintop I realized that He had a plan and a purpose for my life. Walking with Him began to calm the raging storm within me, which gave me clarity to see that the joy of the Kingdom lay on the other side of the comforts of this world!

As we drove into Franconia Notch State Park, in New Hampshire, the sky was crystal clear as His mercy rose with the shining of the morning sun. The beautiful light of day radiated upon the trees as the wind gently blew through them within the notch, personifying them as they clapped, singing His praises. It was early May in the

Northeast, and in the higher elevations of the White Mountains were the familiar scenes of winter of snow and ice. It was cold!

Our destination was to summit the 5,260-foot mountain. This journey would be via the Bridle Path trail, which follows a western spur ridge of Lafayette, from Lafayette Place Campground on Interstate 93, past the Greenleaf AMC Hut, joining the Greenleaf Trail, and ultimately reaching the summit a short distance after the hut.

Up the mountain I went, to my destiny moment!

We finished lunch with a couple of other hikers on the back deck of the AMC hut and began our final ascent. It was getting colder, and we began putting on warmer gear as we navigated through more snow and ice. With the thinning of the air, the tighter gripping of the cold, and the thickening silence, an overwhelming desire to run ahead came over me. I motioned to my friend that I was going to run up ahead a bit, which he had no issue with. Closing in on the summit, with my heart pounding and my lungs stinging from the cold air, I somehow knew that a milestone of this journey was at hand. I saw a large rock come into view, converging with my path, and I soon found myself standing upon this large rock. It was as if the Lord had gone ahead and had prepared this place of peaceful solitude and comfort so I could clearly hear His voice without all the other distractions. Standing there upon the rock, I took a deep breath, lifted my head to the Heavens, and began to have a conversation with Him. Time relaxed for a moment. It was awesome.

It was here at this place of desolation, on this rock, on this mountain, where He spoke to my heart. Do you want to know what He said to me? He asked me to collect four stones when I got to the top of the mountain. So, standing in my own strength, leaning on my own understanding and ending the tranquil scene He had prepared for me, my response was, "You want me to do what?"

He knew that this would be my reaction, so it was through the wisdom of my friend, whom the Lord blessed me with on this hike, that I was reminded of other events in the Bible that go beyond our own understanding. God caused a donkey to talk to Balaam; asked Gideon to stand before the Midianites with three hundred men and nothing but trumpets, pitchers, and lamps; and asked Moses to strike a rock to get water. After being reminded of such events, picking up four stones didn't seem so strange anymore. I thought if my friend didn't think I was crazy and I knew that he wasn't crazy—I decided that maybe I wasn't crazy after all. When we live by sight, we can only act on what we see, but God sees what we can't. Remembering the words in 2 Corinthians 5:7, that we are to walk by faith and not by sight, I decided to just trust Him and be obedient.

Trust GOD from the bottom of your heart; don't try to figure out everything on your own. Listen for GOD's voice in everything you do, everywhere you go; he's the one who will keep you on track. — Proverbs 3:5, 6 (MSG)

After resting in that place for a bit, my friend and I decided it was time to head up to the summit, and it wasn't long until I had that compelling desire again to run up on ahead of my friend.

Smiling, he said, "Go get those stones."

I have climbed many mountains in the Northeast and I have to admit that Mt. Lafayette is one of the most beautiful and breathtaking places to be. It's my favorite climb. The upper portion of the mountain is located within the alpine zone, which is an area characterized by little vegetation, rock fields, and harsh weather. When you finally make your way to the summit of Mt. Lafayette, you are blessed with a spectacular view of the surrounding area that spans multiple states. You are also greeted with the ruins of a hotel foundation that was once in use many years ago. It was behind the once protective walls of these hotel ruins where I put on my gloves and began to talk to the Lord, because I had no idea what He meant about picking up four stones when there were literally millions all around me.

After some time in prayer, I began to simply walk out in faith around the rocky and desolate mountaintop, picking up random stones amongst the millions of other stones at the top of this mountain. I spent a good thirty minutes or so walking in faith across the summit of this mountain looking for the stones He wanted me to pick up.

With stones in hand, I began my walk back to the foundational ruins to meet up with my friend. Along the way I had an overwhelming desire to cast one of the stones away, so I did, right off the side of the mountaintop. I would later learn that this act would become a symbolic metaphor of letting go of the baggage I was carrying in my life, such as divorce, my most recent sting of rejection.

Do you see what this means—all these pioneers who blazed the way, all these veterans cheering us on? It means we'd better get on with it. Strip down, start running—and never quit! No extra spiritual fat, no parasitic sins. —Hebrews 12:1 (MSG)

It was cold enough on the mountain top that my breath hung in the air around me. With each step I took, the cold air tightened its grip, slowly eroding what faith I had left. I began wrestling with my thoughts: "Did God really talk to me, or did I somehow convince myself that He did? Seriously, go to the top of the mountain and pick up four stones? There are millions of stones up here…what am I doing? What four stones? What if I don't find them?" As the battle continued in my mind, with a pure act of the will I put aside theology, religion, and what I knew to be real and true. Arriving at the edge of despair, the wonderful and warm thought that God may have really spoken to me began to consume my thoughts. I had to know, I had to take a chance. I had to see if these four stones were real, so with pure faith I continued my hunt for the last and final stone in this surreal game of hide and seek. As if something was guiding me, I stopped, looked down, and picked up a stone, and I somehow knew that this was the final stone. I couldn't explain it, but I knew. The final, fourth stone had taken some time to find because I had to break through the barrier of my own mind, but I had found it!

…a time to cast away stones, and a time to gather stones. —Ecclesiastes 3:5a (MSG)

Well, with my four stones, I headed back over to the foundation ruins to meet back up with my friend. The first thing he asked me was if I had found the stones, and as I opened my hand to reveal the four fractured pieces of stone on the backdrop of my black glove, to our amazement, they somehow fit together. I'm not kidding. These four stones fit together, forming almost a cross like shape when they were joined. I would find it hard to share this story if I did not have my friend as a witness to back it up.

I would later understand that these stones were significant. They would become the process of God that He would use for meaning along my journey.

Waves

This day, the mountaintop experience was a scene painted by the Lord Himself. What I had initially thought was a ridiculous idea swirling around in my head actually turned out to be a place of obedience, a destiny moment of hearing His soft, gentle voice calling me to pick up those four stones and carry them down the mountain. This act of obedience required taking risk. My friend could have thought I was crazy, as others have. It's so much easier to play it safe, stay off the mountains of life and blame others for our current circumstance rather than walk it out with the Lord. If it's been a while since you've seen God work in such a way that you know it was Him, you may not be trusting Him or you may not be risking enough. On our journey toward the heart of God, we will come to that place where trusting in Him and being obedient to His will enables us to see what others cannot see. After that day, I wanted to be done with low living and sight walking. I wanted to go on an adventure with the Lord!

At about four o'clock in the morning, Jesus came toward them walking on the water. —Matthew 14:25 (MSG)

In the movie *The Guardian*, a Coast Guard rescue team goes into a violent, raging sea to rescue a husband and wife from the pounding waves. The team just about has the situation under control when the husband, out of self-preservation, panics and shifts into survival mode, which results in his wife almost drowning and the Coast Guard rescuer having to elbow him in the nose to calm him down. As I was watching this scene, I thought to myself that it must be very difficult to rescue someone panicking in the raging waves of a storm at sea or any situation. What I didn't realize at the time was that this was a foreshadowing of my circumstances.

It was four in the morning and the disciples were up all night fishing; we read in the fourteenth chapter of Matthew that a fierce wind came up against them, and they became battered, tossed, and beaten down by the waves around them. This storm must have brought them to the point of exhaustion. Then Jesus does something that absolutely blows their minds. He comes walking toward them on the water right in the middle of the storm. Could you have imagined the thoughts of the disciples during this scene?

We read that they literally freaked out.

When we freak out we cannot see our destination, but God can.

We think we are alone, but we are not.

We often complain when God doesn't show up in the convenience of our time frame, but His timing is perfect. In Ecclesiastes 4:11, we read that "He makes all things beautiful in His time." We all find ourselves in different circumstances in life, but in the same way, I believe that God will allow us to get to the end of ourselves and to the end of our resources, so we will finally stop fighting and panicking and just reach out to Him. Jesus is waiting for us to let go and let Him rescue us, and sometimes that is found on the other side of exhaustion, once we are beaten down by the storm or by an elbow to the face.

When we are going through hardships it is so easy to believe the lie that God has forgotten about us, that He is too busy for us, or that He doesn't love us. I know we question why God chooses to hide Himself during our time of need, but His promises are true, and He will reveal Himself when the time is right. Remember that when someone is hiding, it means that they are there even though you cannot see them at that moment. God loves you more than you could ever imagine, and He knows what you are experiencing. Jesus did not forget the disciples in the boat that night, but He will always come in His time.

At this point the disciples were physically exhausted and beaten down by this storm and they were panicking, fighting for their self-preservation. Jesus then says to them, **"Don't be afraid."** Suddenly the consuming waves around them, beating them down, fade into the distance as they look upon the face of Jesus. They begin to stop panicking and begin to trust. In fact, we read that Peter suddenly gets bold, steps out of the boat and begins to walk toward Jesus on the water. Still not quite sure about this trusting God thing yet, Peter loses focus on Jesus again, begins to see the waves again, and begins to sink, and he panics. Peter, extending his hand, then cries out to Jesus, and Jesus reaches down and firmly grasps Peter's hand to bring him to safety.

Peter is beginning to get it!

After Peter's walk on the water, the disciples receive Jesus into the boat, and then the storm stops. Did you catch that? The storm stops! Here is the piercing question I would have to ask myself: Would I still trust God even when things didn't go my way? Could I trust God when life didn't go the way that I hoped it would?

When the storms in life surround you, let go and step out of the boat onto the crashing waves to a surface you have no business being on; it will become a rite of passage for anyone willing to take risk. It's not easy to stop focusing on the waves and to trust God, but take a look at your current circumstances. What's the alternative? Try it. Step out of the boat, climb the mountain, pick up four stones…whatever it is God is calling you to do—do it! What have you got to lose?

Before we leave this awesome scene, let's not forget that earlier that day, Jesus intentionally asks the disciples to get in the boat and to go ahead to the other side of the sea. I don't know if you caught that, but Jesus knew that the storm would come. It is because of God's perfect timing and His incredible love for us that He sometimes will go to extreme measures to get our attention. Although they may have lost sight of Jesus, He never lost sight of them. Our struggles, hardships, and disappointments can lead to a divine appointment with the Lord, just like the scene of the boat. I am learning that it's better to be in a storm with Jesus than anywhere else without Him.

Symbols

When we begin to explore God's word, it doesn't take too long to discover that God uses tangible symbols as a way of communicating to us. Often God's people are instructed to make use of symbols to help them understand or remember what God is teaching them. Some examples of symbols include

- the rainbow as the sign of God's covenant to us that He will never again destroy the earth by a flood (Genesis 9:13),
- the placement of the twelve stones in the River Jordan to remind the Israelites of the crossing God had provided for them "as a sign" and "memorial" (Joshua 4:3-7),
- the star of Bethlehem to signify the birth of Christ (Matthew 2:2),
- the dove to signify the Spirit's presence at Jesus' baptism (John 1:32),
- water to signify one's commitment to Christ at baptism (Romans 6:4),
- bread and wine to signify Jesus' body and blood (1 Corinthians 11:23-26),
- the symbol of a lamb to represent Jesus Christ (John 1:29), and
- *my heartstone* (Joshua 24:27 NLT).

Also, we still use symbols today to communicate important moments of significance such as wedding rings, birthday cakes, birth stones, and red roses. They are used today as a natural way of communicating significant meaning. There are also many references to the symbolism of stones in the bible, but here are some that I have collected that have significance for me.

Stones were widely used as building materials to build walls:

The wall was finished on the twenty-fifth day of Elul. It had taken fifty-two days. When all our enemies heard the news and all the surrounding nations saw it, our enemies totally lost their nerve. They knew that God was behind this work.—Nehemiah 6:15, 16 (MSG)

Jesus Christ is our "Cornerstone":

Jesus said, "Right—and you can read it for yourselves in your Bibles: The stone the masons threw out is now the cornerstone. This is God's work; we rub our eyes, we can hardly believe it! 'This is the way it is with you. God's kingdom will be taken back from you and handed over to a people who will live out a kingdom life. Whoever stumbles on this Stone gets shattered; whoever the Stone falls on gets smashed. —Matthew 21:42-44 (MSG)

Stones were used as weapons for protection:

The Four Stones

Here on my knees I cry out to You, my Lord.
Tear-stained, wounded by the choices I have made
Seeking the world's view of success, coveting the award.
Got what I wanted; the dream shatters; it begins to fade.

Self-righteousness and pride, thinking I had all the answers.
Never giving in. Always my way; never able to compromise.
Convinced I could work things out…coming to my end, I admit I was wrong!
Needing a completing love, desiring to be whole, Lord, help me to rise!

Don't love the world's ways. Don't love the world's goods. Love of the world squeezes out love for the Father. —1 John 2:15 (MSG)

This bitter darkness surrounds me, feeling so alone.
Reaching out for Him, faced with this choice now,
Again I cry out to Him, asking Him, How?
With a gentle whisper I hear, "Just remove the stone!"

With nothing left, I surrender…

Searching for my way, giving it my all, I try.

I could never be this strong without You, I need You at my side!
Stumbling, trying to find my way; without You I am lost.
Now I know; I am nothing without You, my Adonai.

Your light begins to shine; it surrounds me,
Broken and humbled; You change me, restoring my spirit!
Never judging me for my faults, just unconditionally loving me,
My Jesus, without You I don't know where I'd be.

Please stay with me, guide me through my mistakes.
Holding on to Your promise, knowing You will never leave my side,
I love the way You lift me up, when I stumble, when my heart breaks.
To have You in my life is enough; Spirit of God be my guide!

You are everywhere! You surround me; I can feel your awesome love!
Longing for that day, to embrace the beauty of Your face
Whenever I lose my way, my Abba…You always make it okay!
Shining a light so I can see, blessing me with peace and grace.

You are here with me now and You calm my fears.
Always leading me back with Your gentle sweet song,
I am forever grateful; You've given me so much!
Its the way you lift me up! You're where I belong!

I will serve You forever; follow You with everything I have…

For ye have not received the spirit of bondage again to fear; but ye have received the Spirit of adoption, whereby we cry, Abba, Father. —Romans 8:15 (KJV)

Out of this cold darkness and into the light.
He is here, showing me all of His majesty, all of his might!
He has all the answers; He hears all my prayers.

I know who I am now; He took away all of my cares!

From the shadows of the valley to face these unknowns,
For clarity of thought, My Lord brings me to a mountaintop.
He whispers to me, "My precious one; gather up four stones."
Knowing my path, I will stand, rise up, persevere…I will not STOP!

Hearing the spoken truth, I gather up four stones…

I place the first stone into my hand.

For he hath made him to be sin for us, who knew no sin; that we might be made the righteousness of God in him. —2 Corinthians 5:21 (KJV)

The giant of blame reminds me of all my failures. I place this first stone into my sling! By faith, I aim, and I fire! I am the righteousness of God!

I place the second stone into my hand.

With the arrival of Jesus, the Messiah, that fateful dilemma is resolved. Those who enter into Christ's being-here-for-us no longer have to live under a continuous, low-lying black cloud. A new power is in operation. The Spirit of life in Christ, like a strong wind, has magnificently cleared the air, freeing you from a fated lifetime of brutal tyranny at the hands of sin and death. —Romans 8:1, 2 (MSG)

My Abba poured out His love on Calvary! Through the sacrifice of Jesus the law of the Spirit of life has set me free from the law of sin and death. I place the second stone into my sling! By faith, I aim, and I fire! Jesus has set me free!
I place the third stone into my hand.

Give your entire attention to what God is doing right now, and don't get worked up about what may or may not happen tomorrow. God will help you deal with whatever hard things come up when the time comes. —Mathew 6:34 (MSG)

Hope gives us strength to rest in our Father's arms, where He completely consumes all of our worries of tomorrow. Psalms 46:10, "Be still, and know that I am God: I will be exalted among the heathen, I will be exalted in the earth."

I place the third stone into my sling! By faith, I aim, and I fire! He is God!

I place the fourth stone into my hand.

Christ arrives right on time to make this happen. He didn't, and doesn't, wait for us to get ready. He presented himself for this sacrificial death when we were far too weak and rebellious to do anything to get ourselves ready. And even if we hadn't been so weak, we wouldn't have known what to do anyway. We can understand someone dying for a person worth dying for, and we can understand how someone good and noble could inspire us to selfless sacrifice. —Romans 5:6, 7 (MSG)

Self is the biggest giant we face! We must deny ourselves! Lay all of your cares at the feet of Jesus. Then rise up, turn and walk away; without giving it a second thought.

I place the fourth stone into my sling! By faith, I aim, and I fire! I give you my all! I will serve You forever!

"Then said David to the Philistine, Thou comest to me with a sword, and with a spear, and with a shield: but I come to thee in the name of the LORD of hosts, the God of the armies of Israel, whom thou hast defied. This day will the LORD deliver thee into mine hand; and I will smite thee, and take thine head from thee; and I will give the carcasses of the host of the Philistines this day unto the fowls of the air, and to the wild beasts of the earth; that all the earth may know that there is a God in Israel. And all this assembly shall know that the LORD saveth not with sword and spear: for the battle is the LORD's, and he will give you into our hands. And it came to pass, when the

Philistine arose, and came and drew nigh to meet David, that David hasted, and ran toward the army to meet the Philistine. And David put his hand in his bag, and took thence a stone, and slung it, and smote the Philistine in his forehead, that the stone sunk into his forehead; and he fell upon his face to the earth. So David prevailed over the Philistine with a sling and with a stone, and smote the Philistine, and slew him; but there was no sword in the hand of David. —1 Samuel 17:45-50 (KJV)

Do not fear the unknown! He is here with you; you're not alone!
God heals you when you're broken!
Let Him In! Standing at the door waiting; He waits for it to open!

I've told you all this so that trusting me, you will be unshakable and assured, deeply at peace. In this godless world you will continue to experience difficulties. But take heart! I've conquered the world. — John 16:33 (MSG)

My heart of hardened stone finally fractured along its four chambers because of an overexposure to the "truth" and an under response to the Truth. With tears running down my face, I would hold out the four fractured pieces of stone in the darkness of my hand up into the cold air of that desolate mountaintop as an offering to the Lord—the symbolic pieces of my broken heart.

The sacrifices of God are a broken spirit: a broken and a contrite heart, O God, thou wilt not despise. —Psalms 51:17 (KJV)

"Lord, help me with all these regrets I am carrying! Take these pieces of stone, the scattered pieces of who I am, as the sacrifice of my broken heart and make me whole! I want to get well!"

And I will give them one heart, and I will put a new spirit within you; and I will take the stony heart out of their flesh, and will give them a heart of flesh. —Ezekiel 11:19 (KJV)

Heaven collided with Earth as the fabric of time unstitched itself and stood still as He gently blanketed me with a covering of peace. Burdened with all the garbage I collected and carried with me over the years, such as rejection, betrayal, and shame, I couldn't grasp how He could love me so much and why He came to me, but I am so glad He did. I allowed the Lord to break through and invade my life as I soaked in the stillness of His awesome presence on the mountaintop. This was the place where my sorrow collided with the joy of His grace! It was awesome being here with Him, and I wanted to stay longer, but He revealed in my heart that the necessary growth could only take place in the valleys of life and not here on the mountaintop. With a renewed strength, I walked down from the mountaintop with the Lord into the valleys. This is where I would spend more time shedding tears and getting to know myself, and most importantly, getting to know God.

We always have a vision of something before it actually becomes real to us. When we realize that the vision is real, but is not yet real in us, satan comes to us with his temptations, and we are inclined to say that there is no point in even trying to continue. Instead of the vision becoming real to us, we have entered into a valley of humiliation. God gives us a vision, and then He takes us down to the valley to batter us into the shape of that vision. It is in the valley that so many of us give up and faint. Every God-given vision will become real if we will only have patience. Just think of the enormous amount of free time God has! He is never in a hurry. Yet we are always in such a frantic hurry. While still in the light of the glory of the vision, we go right out to do things, but the vision is not yet real in us. God has to take us into the valley and put us through fires and floods to batter us into shape, until we get to the point where He can trust us with the reality of the vision. Ever since God gave us the vision, He has been at work. He is getting us into the shape of the goal He has for us, and yet over and over again we try to escape from the Sculptor's hand in an effort to better ourselves into the shape of our own goal. The vision that God gives is not some unattainable castle in the sky, but a vision of what God wants you to be down here. Allow the Potter to put you on His wheel and whirl you around as He desires. Then as surely as God is God, and you are you, you will turn out as an exact likeness of the vision. But don't lose heart in the process. If you ever had a vision from God, you may try as you will to be satisfied on a lower level, but God will never allow it. —Oswald Chambers

These four stones would eventually become my "heap of stones" that I would place in the dry riverbed of my past as a signpost to always remember where I have been. To be blessed with a revelation of God that brings us to a place in our lives where we become completely reliant on the very character of Him becomes the source of our strength and the wellspring of our joy.

The only way we can step into the scene of the vision He has so majestically painted for us is to rest in His very nature, to trust Him, and to see Him for who He really and truly is. And that was just what He had planned for me.

Never be afraid to trust an unknown future to a known God. —Corrie Ten Boom

Somehow a bird's-eye view simply clarifies for us the lay of the land, and sometimes you cannot get this any way other than through divine perspective on the mountaintop. You might come to the conclusion that my life would change instantly, that my sorrows would have been left on that mountain. The reality is that I had to walk through more stuff and it would take years to walk it out. Even though I walk through the darkest valley, God will be with me no matter what. I only fail when I stop trying. With this new perspective, I was ready to quiet my spirit so I could hear the soft, gentle voice of my Heavenly Father sing the dreams He had for me.

God began to heal my sin-sick soul.

Now it was time for Him to redeem it!

Third Stone § Wilderness

Therefore, behold, I will allure her, and bring her into the wilderness, and speak comfortably unto her and I will give her vineyards from thence, and the valley of Achor for a door of hope: and she shall sing there, as in the days of her youth, and as in the day when she came up out of the land of Egypt.
—Hosea 2:14, 15 (KJV)

Hope has two beautiful daughters. Their names are anger and courage; anger at the ways things are, and courage to see that they do not remain the way they are. — Augustine

Delays

...while Saul, picking himself up off the ground, found himself stone blind. They had to take him by the hand and lead him into Damascus. —Acts 9:8 (MSG)

There is a place of obedience for each and every one of us to discover, and one of those places for me began on my mountain of desolation and would continue to be refined out in the wilderness. Paul found this place of obedience on the Damascus road when he was knocked off his horse and struck blind. We find in this scene Jesus asking Paul why he was persecuting Him and when Paul was able to stand back on his feet, he could not see. Jesus then tells him to go to Damascus and meet a man named Ananias, and it was at that place of grace that Jesus restored Paul's sight through Ananias.

Each of us has a place of obedience. For some of us it requires only a gentle nudge of applied pressure to our circumstances to lead us toward the Lord. For me, it was an elbow to my face—divorce. What will it be for you? God sometimes has to knock us off of our horses for us to gain clarity. If we choose to rise up, God will not keep us in our blindness for long and it was at this place of obedience that Jesus restored Paul's sight.

Running into the wilderness was not my idea.

My friend and his wife graciously let me take up residence in a small corner room of the upstairs of their home for the summer. I was finally moving up in the world, since my last place of residence had been a basement floor. This became a wonderful time of renewal, fellowship, and healing, but the summer was coming to an end. It was time to leave the tiny little room and let my friend have his family's interrupted lives back.

Saddened by the shame of only being able to provide an air mattress for my kids to sleep on, I would spend much time in prayer as well as looking for my next place to stay. Trying to find another apartment was very discouraging, as I did not have the financial resources to afford much, so I began to ask the Lord to show me where He wanted me to move next.

My journey to find another place to call home began with joy and excitement, but quickly turned into one disappointment after another. I was not ready to enter the housing market at this place in my life so I spent most of my time stumbling through many apartment listings in newspapers, online and in those free real-estate magazines you can pick up at restaurants and such. I would soon learn the reality of apartment hunting: apartments were extremely overvalued for what was included; landlords didn't return phone calls; many of the listings were old or already rented. I came to realize that I really didn't want to live in a big red-brick rectangle. I am not sure what apartment complexes look like in your area, but here they come in many styles and jamming as many small apartments into a red-brick cube or rectangle is one of them.

I would spend many nights and weeks in prayer with absolutely no results, and I began to lose sight of the Lord and to focus outwardly on the waves again. I would pray and pray and pray, and still nothing. I had to keep reminding myself that just because finding an apartment had not happened yet didn't mean that it would never happen. I read in a devotional somewhere that God's delays are not necessarily His denials.

Jesus told them a story showing that it was necessary for them to pray consistently and never quit. — *Luke 18:1 (MSG)*

After what seemed an endless pursuit of prayer and empty days draining my hope, I was sitting in the kitchen of my friend's house when his wife handed me a newspaper with a few potential places to check out. One that caught her curiosity was an apartment in Groton, Massachusetts, which was located at an old New England inn. I shrugged it off because it was a rental listing that did not disclose the monthly, rent and I immediately assumed that there was no way I could afford it. After some more discouraging days of no one calling me back, or places being already rented when I called, I decided to call the number on the rental listing in Groton. To my surprise, it was the only time I got a live person on the other end.

The woman on the other end of the phone initially spoke with a monotone voice, but after answering her many questions, she became more animated. She was thrilled that I had two kids and was excited to share with me that they would love the in-ground pool in the summertime. So without delay, she wanted me to come by the inn and meet the landlord in person. When I arrived the next day, she greeted me in the parking lot and guided me into the inn where we sought out the landlord. After wandering the halls for a bit I finally came face-to-face with an older man who began an informal interview process with me. What happened next took me by surprise. He didn't ask to see any references or my credit history; he simply smiled and rented me the apartment.

That day I stepped into another miracle of God's awesome grace as the landlord graciously provided me the place without any questions and for a price I could afford. I will never forget what he said to me: "There is something honest in your eyes…I will rent you the place, and do not worry about last month's rent or utilities."

I was starting to understand God's delays.

I was so excited with the news that I had an apartment that I went back to the police station where my friend worked to share the story. Just when I thought God was finished, my friend went on to tell me that he and his wife were going to provide me with a bed, a microwave, a kitchen table with chairs, drinking glasses, and a complete twelve-piece dish set for a home-warming gift. Sinking back in my chair, I brought my hands up to my face and began to weep right there in the police station. Later that week, other people provided me with other necessities, free, as gifts!

"Thank you, God."

Giving you the things that you need in your life brings joy for God. Have you found yourself at a place where you have been praying for something for awhile with no answer? Maybe there is a delay for a reason. When we experience these delays in our life, they are not always easy to handle and are typically difficult to understand.

Also, when God does not show up according to our timeline of instant gratification, we often entertain a false reality to the character of God's nature and believe the lie that He does not care. God often has to delay His work in us in order to accomplish something for His purposes that can only be achieved by the delay. Maybe we should take on the perspective that all the delays we experience in life are actually God's intervention.

Test

A long season has passed since I had to leave the comfort of my own home. This journey was humbling as I had to walk through the transient way of life from a basement floor, to the top of a barn, to a single room, to this apartment that the Lord blessed me with. Walking this out, I arrived to a place that represented some sense of emotional and financial stability where I could stand on my own and have my own place.

There was a calming stillness to the morning air as I walked out of my friend's garage to the scene of him and my father hooking up the trailer. The scene unfolded in slow motion as I was beginning the journey to be on my own. As the sun began to chase away the clouds, we began to load what little personal items I had on to the back of a trailer. This didn't take long because I did not have much to move. With the last of everything I owned loaded onto the trailer, we began the trip to my new apartment. My emotions were mixed with excitement and anxiety because not only was this a big step that would bring closure to my transient life, but thoughts began to stir in my head reminding me that I would truly be on my own.

We walked into the emptiness of the apartment, quickly made a decision on where everything should go and began the process of unloading and unpacking all my stuff. The emptiness of the apartment slowly retreated as each item was put in its place. It was really great hanging out with my buddy and my father through the rest of that day; but the day came to a close, night began to blanket the sky, and they headed home.

I was alone…again!

I really thought I conquered fear and loneliness, but I hadn't.

Time appeared to slow as I watched them get in their vehicles and drive off. Watching the scene fade as I closed the door, I walked back into the apartment with an ache developing in the pit of my stomach. Within minutes, the silence and loneliness began to consume me as I sat there at my kitchen table staring at the wall.

My thoughts churned into knots as I began to wonder why God would bless me with this apartment and would graciously provide me all the necessities I needed to exist here, just to leave me all alone. It didn't take me long before this scene reminded me what it was like living in my own house, with all my stuff, despite the issues. My anger and my pride began to rise up within me as I thought how absolutely stupid it was to be in this small apartment at the back of an inn with no couch, no TV, no Internet access, no curtains, no shades, and little to eat.

Why me?

I worked for years to have that house!

Why me and not her!

My excitement turned to disappointment!

My disappointment turned to anger.

Through His incredible grace, God had provided me with so much that I couldn't see at the time. This was that place on my journey into the mystery of God where He stepped back into the silence and tested me to see what I would do, similar to how our parents teaching us how to walk by holding our hands for a time and then letting go to see what we will do.

I have learned that as we journey with God, He will allow us to experience the disappointment we feel when our pride is wounded. It is in this place where our misplaced affections and desires will be clearly revealed to us, whether we like it or not. Because of our stubbornness and our pride, we cannot clearly see that these are the very things that can only be worked out in us when He gets us alone—and because He loves us so much, He will get us alone. Take it from me, the Lord cannot teach us anything until we throw away our human wisdom and thinking and get alone with Him, and when He gets us alone, these issues will become clearer to us.

There are times of transition when God may decide to hide Himself, and in this hiddenness, we are called to action. When God chooses to hide Himself amid our circumstances and the silence becomes deafening, we will find over time that He was always there with us. He hides to invite us into a deeper intimacy. This silence is not a silence of despair, but a silence of pleasure; it's an opportunity to really get to know Him. Remember, when God chooses to hide Himself He has not left us—to be hidden means that He is still there, just not easily seen. God will always look deep into our hearts to see the substance of who we are and it is there that He determines if we can handle an even greater revelation. So if God has blessed you with silence, then find the will to lift your hands toward the Heavens and praise Him. It is an invitation to rediscover the Living God and it is quite possibly the beginning of Him bringing you into the mainstream of His purposes.

I soon would come to realize that it was in this lonely wilderness place where He would reveal some major stumbling blocks in my life: my foolish and stubborn pride. God absolutely hates pride, and it consumed me to the core! In the gospel of Mark, it's unmistakably clear that pride defiles us[iii]. Proverbs sums it up simply for us; *every one that is proud in heart is an abomination to the LORD: though hand join in hand, he shall not be unpunished.[iv]* I came to the difficult realization that it was necessary for the Lord to allow me to get to this place of emptiness before He could begin the rebuilding process. Restoration was His plan, but He had much work ahead of Him!

If you puff yourself up, you'll get the wind knocked out of you. But if you're content to simply be yourself, your life will count for plenty. —Matthew 23:12 (MSG)

What is truly awesome is that no matter how much we have failed or messed up, God still accepts us and sees us for who we really are. I do not know if I will ever fully understand why He loves us so much and why He holds us the way He does, broken as we are, but He does. He will restore us to His full inheritance if we will just let Him capture our hearts and yield to Him, because He is a God of redemption and He will redeem what we place in His hands!

> We can be slow to learn that what causes the most pain is not the initial loss or hardship but the failure to learn anything in the process. If we really believe that God is working all things for our good, then one of the great challenges is to allow hard, painful, and tear-filled experiences to be our teacher in the classroom of life.[v]

Adjusting to this new life in this wilderness was difficult. The hardship of divorce that appeared to have no end in sight, the doubts of all these circumstances eroding my very will to move forward and the pain of watching my children caught in the middle of this tragedy consumed me. I realized that I had to choose between allowing these hardships and tribulations to numb my very existence or letting go and faithfully trusting that God was there walking with me and helping me, despite the outward circumstances which seemed to smash me through the hard realities of life.

Corners

In my wilderness, the Lord provided me with the much-needed manna from Heaven, but just as the Israelites did, I began to grumble, my vision started to fade, and I began to panic. I would visibly see the awesome hand of God working in my life all around me, then the very next day enter into the passivity of life and retreat to my golden calf. You know…our idols. Those things we have to consult with before we acknowledge God.

My self-preservation began to rise up again.

The Israelites did it, and now I was doing it!

Why do we do this?

What the heck?

I soon began to run the spectrum from patience to aggravation as I became more and more tormented by a leak in the roof of my apartment, which seemed to never stop. This was no ordinary leak; it was witty, because every time we thought we had stopped it, it would show itself again with a vengeance. After grumbling to the landlord, the kids, my friends, and anyone else who would listen, frustration won the battle in my mind, and I began to allow the tentacles of self-pity to slowly wrap around me. In my impulse to fix this myself, I sank further into the pit of self-pity, and glimpses of hope began to slowly fade.

How could a leak consume and cripple me?

A leak in a roof may sound like a silly problem, but we all allow these little things to become giants in our lives. It was actually driving me crazy because I couldn't fix it. We have bought into a culture that demands an instant fix and that convinces us that our way is the best way! Over time, this becomes an automatic response, like breathing, and we blindly strive to satisfy this intense, cultural lie. This striving robbed me of my ability to rest and enjoy life's moments, and for much of my life, I struggled with this. No matter what I did or where I went, something would entangle me and pull me into restlessness. I would later learn through months of counseling that I was stuck in a pattern of trying to fix the relationship between my mom and my dad, a kid still believing that somehow I could still fix it. This pattern became so embedded in my psyche that I convinced myself that if I couldn't fix their relationship, it somehow made me a failure. God will never give up on us because He loves us—we are the ones who give up on Him! I'm glad I didn't give up.

Days faded in and out as God continued pursuing me, trying to get my attention, but I didn't want to listen, and I decided to handle things myself for a bit. I spent the days ahead striving on my own, but enough time and circumstances went by, eroding my stubbornness along the way that I was ready to listen again. I was still learning to trust Him.

It appeared to be just another day walking to the mailbox to get my mail, but God had other plans. As I began to sort through it all; junk, bills, attorney letters (I really didn't like those), I came to my monthly newsletter from Shiloh Place Ministries, which caught my attention. On the front page in big bold letters was an article with the title, "When We Strive, God Waits; When We Rest, God Acts" by Jack Frost. Funny how God works, isn't it?

> A competitive culture tends to define rest as a place of idleness or being unproductive. But Biblical rest is not a place without activity or fruitfulness. Rest is a posture of the heart that feels so sheltered in God's love that it does not allow itself to be pulled into a place where we strive to feel valued, affirmed, or secure.[vi]

Reading this article was a breakthrough moment for me and it offered me to see my circumstances through a different lens. God was teaching me that when we strive, He rests, and when we rest…He acts!

Striving in my life always resulted in grumbling.

I was grumbling just like the Israelites in the wilderness.

I was exhausted.

I began to understand that the manna was for survival and symbolic of His daily provisions. Walking this out in real life is difficult, because it demands trusting Him no matter what our circumstances look like. We have a choice to pursue our destiny in Him or stand back and allow circumstances to define who we are—so many of us think that God will bring the Promised Land to us.

He did not bring the Promised Land across the Red Sea to the Israelites.

He did not bring the Promised Land to Joshua before the battles.

God will lead us, guide us, fight for us, and give us the strength to get there, but we must find rest in Him to move forward and stop striving to allow Him to act. Learning to rest in Him is a process, a long process. Life still presents me with opportunities to see how rested I am in Him, how about you?

> 1 Peter 4:12 says, Beloved, do not think it strange concerning the fiery trial which is to try you, as though some strange thing happened to you…Rise to the occasion—do what the trial demands of you. It does not matter how much it hurts as long as it gives God the opportunity to manifest the life of Jesus in your body. May God not find complaints in us anymore, but spiritual vitality—a readiness to face anything He brings our way. —Oswald Chambers

Have you ever tried to wrap yourself around Proverbs 14:12, which reads, *"There is a way that seems right to a man, but in the end it leads to death?"* In the book of Lamentations, Jeremiah saw God pushing him to despair before revealing joy and goodness. This is where I came into direct conflict with that piece of Scripture, because as Jeremiah experienced, God loves us enough to get us into that corner in order to make us face our absolute misery. It is in that corner that we will have to confront the deep empty darkness of our misery until we can truly appreciate the comfort and the value of the His light. I began to see a ray of hope in all the circumstances that were surrounding me.

If he works severely, he also works tenderly. His stockpiles of loyal love are immense. He takes no pleasure in making life hard, in throwing roadblocks in the way—Lamentations 3:32, 33 (MSG)

He caught my attention again when my cousin handed me a book by Anne Graham Lotz called "*Why?*" (W Publishing Group, 2004), which was another miracle because I wrestled with that question almost on a daily basis. Within this revelation, the author used the story of Jesus raising Lazarus from the dead as the binding theme throughout the book. Lazarus was sick and Jesus was sent for. He did not come right away, and when He arrived upon the scene, one could have just imagined what Martha was thinking because Lazarus had been in the tomb for four days. In John 11:39; Jesus simply said, "**Remove the stone**." The Lord used the message in this book to help me better understand that I needed to stop striving and resisting the process. The stone represented not only the misery of my circumstances, but also my pride. I had to find a way to remove the stone so I could move forward.

How far to the edge do we have to go before we come to a place of surrender in Him?

Lazarus was dead. Thank the Lord I didn't have to walk that path.

In the dark, lonely emptiness of this corner, I arrived to a place of surrender. Wanting this stone to be removed, I cried out to the Lord, "Heavenly Father, please remove the stone and set me free. I want to come home!"

The deep desire of my heart to want to come home to Him finally overshadowed the anguish and misery of my circumstances. I didn't fully understand what I was asking at the time, but I wanted Him to conquer the stronghold of my heart. Walking it out over time, I have learned that this was a buckle-your-seat-belt request, but today I find myself asking God what He is trying to teach me instead of why is this happening to me.

I am the vine; you are the branches. If a man remains in me and I in him, he will bear much fruit; apart from me you can do nothing. —John 15:5 (NIV)

> The words home-home tell us a little of what Jesus was meaning when He said, "…apart from Me…nothing." He wants to be our home-home. Not our summer place, not our vacation retreat, not somewhere we go from time to time, but the place we are when we want to be home-home. He is saying that we will never be at home until we are at home in Him. For there is no life apart from the source of life and He is the source. When He says "apart from Me," He is not just talking about what we do. He is asking us where we live. [vii]

Prodigal

Leaving the story of Lazarus, let's jump into the story of the prodigal son. I found myself in the squalor of my own "pig slop" just as the prodigal son did. I had to stray far so I could begin to understand that the recklessness of my choice to have "my portion" right now placed me in ruins. I had foolishly pursued many temporary things such as wealth, power, and success. With a present-tense gratification, without any care or concern about my future—my selfish nature wanted it now!

As this prodigal son journeys home, covered with the muddy filth and stench of the pig's squalor and gets closer to his father's house, the more his heart begins to beat at the thought of having to face his father. Something strange begins to unfold within this scene of anxious desperation; the father is actually anticipating his return and runs toward his broken, filth-covered son. The father does not respond to what the son had done, but according to his own loving heart as a father. This is the same way God acts toward us when we run back to Him. The father loves his son more than he could ever have imagined, and the same love that received him as a son enables him to enter the house again as a son. The servants are sent to find the best robe and put it on the son; in our wretchedness, we are clothed with Jesus when we enter the Father's house, which is just awesome! This is Heaven's best robe, Heaven's best love, Heaven's most incredible grace; it is God Himself and He offers Himself as a gift to everyone!

Are you tired? Worn out? Burned out on religion? Come to me. Get away with me and you'll recover your life. I'll show you how to take a real rest. Walk with me and work with me—watch how I do it. Learn the unforced rhythms of grace. I won't lay anything heavy or ill-fitting on you. Keep company with me and you'll learn to live freely and lightly." —Matthew 11:28–30 (MSG)

God wanted to take all the years of pain, failures, trials, rejections, betrayals, circumstances, anger, nonforgiveness, regrets, and bitterness and weave it all together into something good and beautiful. Piercing through the darkness the Lord gently whispered to my heart, **"I am the God who created you and I am the God who loves you more than you can imagine! My precious**

child, place your life in My hands and let Me take all the heavy burdens that are weighing you down. I want to carry you away to a place only found through My winds of change. I want to show you how to live!"

The tough reality is that God will allow us to be in these dark places so we will draw near to Him and to learn to trust Him with everything we have in us; in fact, it's all we can do to survive. As difficult and as lonely this place was, I soon started to see it as a gift. I would have to walk through other dark places, and I am sure there will be more, but instead of being defeated by them they were used to further define and reveal the person He created me to be.

Journeying through these difficult places I discovered that I had to find a way to choose joy through hope rather than through despair. It was through these places that I discovered that I had to choose patience and endurance through the hardship. It was through these places that I realized I had to choose to be faithful. These are all decisions of the will and I had to find a way to trust Him more.

This is the true joy in life, the being used for a purpose recognized by yourself as a mighty one; the being thoroughly worn out before you are thrown on the scrap heap; the being a force of Nature instead of a feverish selfish little clod of ailments and grievances complaining that the world will not devote itself to making you happy. — George Bernard Shaw

Coming to a place of surrender allows the Spirit of God to jump into our circumstances and give us the strength to walk it out. There are distractions coming at us in IMAX, that left unchecked will erode our desire to finish the journey. It is through His help that enables us to push through with a confidence that is completely foreign to a world lost in darkness. I began to feel more comfortable walking in these places of surrender with the Lord, which was not easy for me because I was a person who needed to be in control of everything. God and I still wrestle with this, but the good news is that He is winning more.

God wanted to cultivate and make fertile the barren fields of my heart, but they were covered in weeds. He went into His shed, pulled out some Weed-B-Gon and started the process of eradicating the weeds that were choking the life out of me. If these weeds had names, they would be called control, unresolved anger, nonforgiveness, bitterness, failure, and rejection. What are the names of your weeds?

Many of the smaller weeds came out without much effort, but there were some big ugly ones that would require much time, effort and pain to fully extract.

> Patience means more than endurance—more than simply holding on until the end. A saint's life is in the hands of God like a bow and arrow in the hands of an archer. God is aiming at something the saint cannot see, but our Lord continues to stretch and strain, and every once in awhile the saint says—I cannot take any more. But God goes on stretching until His purpose is in sight, and then He lets the arrow fly. —Oswald Chambers

The light of the Lord continued to pierce the strongholds of my darkness that I kept hidden so deep within me; areas so hidden they were not totally evident, a side of me that I so deeply suppressed or perhaps refused to acknowledge. I wrestled with my past, marriage, the husband-wife relationship, the relationship with my children, relationships with others, acceptance, and an all-consuming drive to attain money, power, and success. Over time, I would sacrifice her and my children at these very altars. The extent of my brokenness was beyond belief, and the Lord was the only one who could penetrate deep within to heal and restore me from the inside out.

I became a prisoner of the very strongholds that had been erected since childhood, through the trials, the deep pain, the consuming fears, the fierce storms, and the circumstances of life. In a desperate effort to escape the turbulence of life I learned to fill these deficits of unmet love with counterfeit affections. Living a life consumed by the pleasures of this world only results in a life of pain. The Lord revealed to me an important truth: the enemy has the right of traffic in these areas of darkness, and most of us have them from all of our wounding and hurts. My whole life I was simply crying out for the need to be accepted, to be loved unconditionally, to be secure, the need to feel valued (self-worth) and the need to make a meaningful contribution to God's world (significance)!

This wide-road culture of the world promises to make everything as wonderful and beautiful as it can be, but when we foolishly choose this path, we eventually come to a place in our search for meaning where all we find is a deep emptiness.

What a heavy burden God has laid on men! I have seen all the things that are done under the sun; all of them are meaningless, a chasing after the wind. —Ecclesiastes 1:13, 14 (NIV)

The Samaritan woman at the well symbolizes all of us who have used their best efforts to satisfy the yearning for love and completion but find a deep emptiness in the false gratification of counterfeit affections. Until we find rest in the embrace of God's awesome love and are held by His grace, the sense of emptiness that eats away at us will never be satisfied, and nothing we do no matter how much we try will fill this emptiness on our own. God created us to be in relationship with Him, to honor, worship, and glorify Him; no other act of adoration toward the opposite sex, worldly position, possessions, work, or money can bring a sense of long-term pleasure and purpose to our lives. He is the only thing that is pure and true in this world, and He is the one who can meet all of our needs.

I began to learn that we can only function effectively to the degree at which these needs in our lives are met. If these needs are not met, our ability to function as a person becomes greatly affected; however, our needs for love, security, value, and significance can be fully met only in a close and ongoing relationship with the Lord. Although I did not realize it, this is what draws many of us toward a marriage relationship, because we see the possibility of having our needs met through our marriage partner. There is not one person who walks this earth, however loving, kind, and considerate they may be, who can meet all these needs, and sadly over time, our marriage anecdotally becomes two ticks with no dog.

When we turn from Him to find our needs met in the pleasures and satisfaction from this world, we essentially are placing other gods before Him. A place where this shows up in scripture is the message God delivered to Jeremiah for His wayward people. He uses the metaphor of a cistern, which is a receptacle for holding liquids, usually water, and when it becomes fractured or broken and springs a leak, it can no longer hold water anymore. God is saying that if we go out there to the world and drink from that well, it is not going to satisfy us!

…They have forsaken me, the spring of living water, and have dug their own cisterns, broken cisterns that cannot hold water. —Jeremiah 2:13b (NIV)

Stumbles

The process of identifying the stuff that needs to die in us begins in our own garden of Gethsemane: becoming crucified with Christ; letting our former selves die; becoming a new creation in Him, a birth and a resurrection. This is the process that most of us will fight and wrestle with and where most of us give up and not let the Lord complete the process. We have to surrender to Him completely during this time for only He will give us strength to go to the cross, to be crucified with Him and to be resurrected with Him as the old self dies.

> …Do you continue to go with Jesus? The way lies through Gethsemane, through the city gate, outside the camp; the way lies alone, and the way lies until there is no trace of a footstep left, only the voice, "Follow Me." —Oswald Chambers

It's critical to understand that whenever God begins this process in someone's life, He has others standing by to help you on your journey. I have learned that God uses a community of people around us to head off our desire to give up. Remember the journey for Saul who later was given the new name of Paul? God placed Ananias in his life.

How seemingly random to our human understanding these events can be. If you were a Christian back in that time, the name "Saul" would bring out some strong emotions in you as he was the guy whose view of Christianity was to have everyone involved arrested and destroyed. Then one day while on the job of continued persecution of Christians, he finds himself surrounded by a bright light as he was nearing Damascus. He gets knocked off his horse, and the Lord says, **"Saul, Saul, why do you persecute Me?"**

How does a guy like Saul actually answer a question like that?

How do we answer that question?

Saul had been knocked off his horse, had some straight talk with the Lord, was blinded and then the Lord told him to head into the city. Just a normal day—right? While this was all unfolding, a disciple named Ananias, in Damascus, had a vision from the Lord that told him to go find Saul of Tarsus, put his hands on him and Saul will receive sight.

Ananias, knowing who this man was, said, "You want me to do what?"

Ananias found it unbelievable that Saul really could have changed. Knowing his history of persecuting Christians the Lord had to convince him that it was a divine reality. These seemingly random events, perfectly unfolded by the Lord, led to the transformation in a man from Saul to Paul, who became radically and passionately committed to spreading the gospel of Jesus Christ.

We all have these experiences along our journey into the heart of God, whether we realize it or not. I have come to call these divine appointments and events that the Lord orchestrates simply—God stumbles. I am not suggesting that God stumbles, I am simply suggesting this as a play-on-words that attempts to capture the essence of the seemingly unconnected and random events in our lives that the Lord divinely knits together to work out His plan in us. Remember, He sees the beginning and the end.

Let me share one of these events. I was invited to a Christian event that a family member was running on the commons of Lawrence, Massachusetts, and unbeknownst to me, my uncle had pulled up in his truck and joined us. I had not seen my uncle in years, and I had no idea that he would show up at this event. We all shared some awesome fellowship in the Lord that day, and many people stopped to hear the good news of the gospel. As the events of the day were winding down, my uncle and I sat on a stone wall and began to catch up with each other filling in the many gaps over the years. I began to share with him the trials of my divorce and that through this and other life circumstances the Lord was rewriting the pages of my heart.

I had been living a life that was not in relationship with the Lord. I was knocked off my horse when I was handed that letter of divorce, and then I was divinely united with my Ananias. Although the blindness was not immediately removed from my eyes, this began an incredible new season in my life where my uncle would provide the friendship, guidance and advice I needed. I had no idea that during this white space of time the Lord was doing some incredible work in my Uncle's life. The Lord had healed the shame of his past and it was during this season of my journey, my uncle revealed to me a tragic "life-altering" event that happened to him at the age of ten—the deep anguish of being abused as a child in the darkest of ways. I could not believe what I was hearing, and I couldn't believe it could be possible.

The Lord orchestrated these events and brought others into my life that would provide the comforting words, strength, and encouragement I so desperately needed. These same people would help me carry my cross when I couldn't during this extremely painful time on my journey. This was a season where the Lord persistently shined His light into the dark crevices of my life exposing the stuff I was hiding. I learned through this process that we can actually use darkness to hide our sin, hurts, faults, fears, and even our failures. When He shines His light into our dark places, stuff gets exposed and brought out into the open. This is when we begin to see the substance of who we are.

Allowing God into our dark places requires some trust, courage, and a bit of humility—all of which I struggled to yield. I spent years hiding stuff in my dark places, and some of that stuff I didn't want exposed. It helped me when someone shared that true humility is seeing yourself the way God sees you. Do you have that perspective?

Before we can speak the truth of His word, He will thrust His sword right into our hearts!

It's extremely important to remember that we do not have the ability to do this in our own strength! We absolutely need God, and we need to allow the people He brings into our lives to surround us! Often our greatest weakness is our inability to truly acknowledge our need for Him.

If we are not positioned right in our relationship to the Lord, we never catch that wind of His Spirit that enables us to sail against the tide of our limitations and circumstances and arrive at our destination. We keep coming back to the same old places, and we never get free. And the ride can get rough and unpleasant. We sometimes lose control and get the feeling that we're sinking. But when we move with the Spirit of God, He never leaves us to wander around where we are. He moves us on to where we are supposed to be. The problem is, we can't move on to where we are supposed to be if we have dropped anchor in the past.[viii]

Have you dropped anchor in your past?

My anchor was sent overboard long ago and was wedged in tight!

A major reason I was stuck in the past and kept the memory alive of the things I had done was that I didn't really believe that God had forgiven me. Not believing God at His word will move us into a place of denial where we cannot accept His forgiveness and when we do this, we will try to make our own atonement in feelings of guilt.

The hard reality of this is that it minimizes what Jesus did on the cross.

Another reason that kept me in the past was spiritual pride. This gripped me and I had way too high of an opinion of myself by asking questions, such as, "How could I have ever done something like that?" Seriously! It is written…we have all fallen short of the glory of God, and I convinced myself that I was the exception.

Another reason and this is a big one: I wasn't able to forgive myself. I found it really hard to forgive myself. Did you know that the world calls this "shame"? Here is the truth of the word of God! Once you confess your stuff to God—that's the end of it. God loves you more than you can imagine and He has forgiven you! Just bring your stuff to Him. He is waiting.

I arrived at another significant crossroad on my journey where the Lord ministered to me deeply as I listened to a CD series that my uncle handed me titled, "Restoring the Father's Love" by Jack Frost. I was in the right place to receive this deep-piercing message and the Spirit of God began to excavate the many ruins scattered about in the landscape of my past. This was one of the seemingly random events that the Lord was slowly knitting together that I couldn't see at the time.

Let's roll the tape forward a bit…

It was a warm, inviting sunny day as I climbed into the sanctuary of my car to begin my journey down to Gillette Stadium in Foxboro, Massachusetts, where the New England Patriots football team plays. Cruising down route 495 south with light traffic, no distractions, and dressed to impress in my business suit, I became lost in the reflections of the past week. Of course I was also thinking about how awesome it was to have this opportunity of attending an executive breakfast in the visitor's locker room to hear Bill Belichick, the head coach of the New England Patriots speak. There was a welcoming peace that day in the comfort of my car that I was all too enthusiastic to embrace. In the peaceful silence, I was prompted to listen to one of the CD's in the "Restoring the Father's Love" series again.

I came to a place in the series where time stood still, my heart stopped, and my body went completely numb as the existence of the highway and the other cars around me simply faded into the background; I cannot truly explain what happened. My life began replaying right before my eyes as the Spirit of God brought me back into my past and unearthed something that I had suppressed deep within me for most of my life; I, too, had been abused at the age of ten. I wept all the way to my destination.

> During trials we need to continue to stand in His grace. We need to focus on how much He loves us and accepts us for who we are. Nothing we do will make Him love us less. I have found that we must not blame others when everything around us crumbles, but allow the circumstances to be an opportunity for His love to both purify and cleanse our soul from all the bitterness, resentment and anger that we carry. When we get to this place, and it is not easy, we will then begin to experience His awesome love embracing us, which removes the fears, limitations and hindrances of the past. — Jack Frost

This was a big turning point in my life where the Lord would go deeper with my healing. He began the restoration process of removing the places in my life that I used to hide behind because of fear and shame. This undercurrent of fear and shame consumed me and played out in everything I did, even though I thought I had shoved it down far enough. This was a very hard place in my life to visit again, but the Lord gave me the strength and courage to face it head on. I want to share with you the deep hurts I had to walk through in a poem I was inspired to write called "My Hiding Place." Maybe you too will find yourself buried somewhere in these words.

My Hiding Place

This little boy in the world of the indefinite.
Wanting so much to be both accepted and loved.
Looking for my father; he was not to be found.
Accepting my life as an onlooker; watching others embraced by the love of the father.

Looking for love and acceptance.
Wanting so much to find love, to be loved.
Learning that acceptance is unavailable, loneliness takes hold.
Out of fear, I run to my hiding place! Where is my warm embrace?

This little boy in the world of disappointment.
Having a desire to fit in; to be accepted by others.
Looking for my father; he was not to be found.
Accepting my life as a failure, I so much want to be recognized! Watching others hit a ball out of the park, being praised for it.

Looking for love and acceptance.
My hope for acceptance fading, I begin to get used to this.
Out of fear, I run to my hiding place! Where is my warm embrace?

This little boy in the world of evil.

Craving that someone would just accept me! That someone would love me!
At an impressionable age, I thought it came, but this was not love and this was not acceptance! It was a cancer that devoured me from within.
Looking for my father; he was not to be found.
Finally realizing that there is no love and acceptance!

Looking for love and acceptance.
Wanting to be somebody, needing to fill this void.
Out of fear, I run to my hiding place! Where is my warm embrace?

So desperately wanting to be somebody; to be loved, to be accepted.
Control, drive, money, success…POWER!
How easily I discovered a means to fill this void.
"The only way to be a somebody is being able to beat everybody else!"
Yet I still lived in fear.
Fear that grew, fear that controlled me, fear that possessed me! But I had the power!

Looking for love and acceptance.
Two words that faded out of my existence.
Out of fear, I run to my hiding place! Where is my warm embrace?

This little boy in the world of opportunity.
Courtship, marriage, having a family, what an incredible opportunity!
My family wanting so much for me to give acceptance, wanting me so much to give love. I did not know how!
I stopped looking for my father; he was nowhere to be found.
I only knew power; I only knew fear. Never understanding love and acceptance!

Looking for love and acceptance.
Unable to understand…
Out of fear, I run to my hiding place! Where is my warm embrace?

This power corrupted me! My world crumbled at the very foundation on which it was built. My very fabric of existence, ripped apart!

Looking for love and acceptance.
I am completely crushed! I run, I run, I run…
Out of fear, I run to my hiding place! Where is my warm embrace?

Left only with fear! No acceptance, no love!
Out of desperation, I cry out to God!
Suddenly, a warm covering of peace comforts me. My spirit begins to heal!
I am accepted—unconditionally; I am loved—unconditionally.
Looking for love and acceptance.
Freely given—without condition!
I come out of my hiding place! Finding a warm embrace!
This little boy now held in the comforting arms of the Father, my Abba Father!
Released from the chains that have bound me!
My fear is gone!

Through life experiences, my understanding that love was a reward for success or service. Love is simply a gift, a gift that is freely given!
I have forgiven my earthly father as my heavenly Father has forgiven me.
I now understand, how to love, how to accept and how to freely give it—unconditionally!

Capturing this in a poem was a big step for me and was only possible while being closely held in the arms of the Lord. As I read these words over and over again, like a skipping record, I came to a place of surrendering baggage I had been carrying for most of my life. Falling to my knees, still clenching the worn-out poem smudged and blurred by every teardrop, I poured more of my heart out to the Lord.

"The tears which I had been holding back streamed down, and I let them flow as freely as they would, making of them a pillow for my heart. On them it rested." – Augustine

"Heavenly Father, I'm worn out. I don't want to carry this stuff anymore. Forgive me for holding on to all this stuff and for building walls around my pain numbing the hurt of rejection. Father, as much as it hurts, thank You for showing me the baggage I've been carrying. I want to forgive those who did not know how to express real love to me. I ask You to restore my emotions to the innocence of being this little boy. I am Yours and You are mine. You are love and I am created for love. I want to be a gift of love to my family and others. Set me free from this."

I gave up freedom in exchange for a false security. Jesus came to set us free and give us life, but freedom always has a cost and it's never free—Jesus going to the cross demonstrates this. He is inviting us into freedom.

I slowly emerged from hiding and started walking out into freedom.

Ripples

It was just another day when, during my long commute to work, I was playing a mental game of Jenga with the pieces of my life; I was interrupted by the scene of a lake along the roadside. I had driven by this lake every day for years, but something was different about the lake that day—it was placid, and the scenery around the lake was perfectly painted upon its surface.

In a moment, slipping into an incredible daydream with my Heavenly Father, time stood still and the world around me faded away. I found myself at the placid shoreline of this lake standing next to Him, embraced by His loving arm resting upon my shoulder, just like a father and son. The Lord began to show me that the scenery I thought was so perfectly reflected on the lake's surface was actually a distorted view of my present reality and that it was time to see through a new lens so that I could pick up anchor from my past and move forward. This would involve seeing the real me and seeing God for who He really and truly is!

He then reached to the ground, picked up a stone and threw it dead center into the middle of the lake, which was easy for Him to do. With a childlike anticipation, I watched the stone soar through the air in slow motion until it disappeared from my sight. The moment of impact arrived as the glasslike surface of the water became disrupted; one ripple after another moved out from the center of lake touching and altering every inch of the lake and every contour of the shoreline.

What I believed to be real was not real at all!

As water reflects a face, so a man's heart reflects the man. —Proverbs 27:19 (NIV)

I was sold on the idea that somehow this world had the answers to my desperate desire to be accepted, valued, and loved. With all of my education and all of the worlds' answers at my fingertips via the Internet and television drowning out the voice of God, I honestly thought I had it all figured out. But my sense of reality was distorted and my life was a mess. Listen to the conversation between Morpheus and Neo from the movie *The Matrix*.

Morpheus: I see it in your eyes. You have the look of a man who accepts what he sees because he is expecting to wake up. Ironically, that's not far from the truth…Do you believe in fate, Neo?

Neo: No.

Morpheus: Why not?

Neo: Because I don't like the idea that I'm not in control of my life.

Morpheus: I know exactly what you mean. Let me tell you why you're here. You're here because you know something. What you know you can't explain, but you feel it. You've felt it your entire life, that there's something wrong with the world. You don't know what it is, but its there, like a splinter in your mind, driving you mad. It is this feeling that has brought you to me. Do you know what I'm talking about?

Neo: The Matrix.

Morpheus: Do you want to know what it is? The Matrix is everywhere. It is all around us. Even now, in this very room. You can see it when you look out your window or when you turn on your television. You can feel it when you go to work… when you go to church… when you pay your taxes. It is the world that has been pulled over your eyes to blind you from the truth.

Neo: What truth?

Morpheus: That you are a slave, Neo. Like everyone else you were born into bondage. Born into a prison that you cannot taste or see or touch. A prison for your mind. Unfortunately, no one can be told what the Matrix is. You have to see it for yourself.

…

Neo: This—This isn't real?

Morpheus: What is real? How do you define real?[ix]

The Matrix is just another sci-fi movie and is not real, but this conversation is a challenge of perspective and reality. Embracing a new perspective is the starting place of discovering the truth of the upside-down reality of God, which viewed through our own worldview lens, challenges us with questions like

What wisdom sacrifices His Son to hang on a cross to end our misery?

What wisdom says that in order to win, we have to lose everything?

Blessed are the poor in spirit, for theirs is the kingdom of heaven?

Blessed are those who mourn, for they will be comforted?

Blessed are the meek, for they will inherit the earth?

Blessed are those who hunger and thirst for righteousness, for they will be filled?

Blessed are the merciful, for they will be shown mercy?

Blessed are the pure in heart, for they will see God?

Blessed are the peacemakers, for they will be called sons of God?

Blessed are those who are persecuted because of righteousness, for theirs is the kingdom of heaven?

Blessed are you when people insult you, persecute you, and falsely say all kinds of evil against you because of Me [God]. Rejoice and be glad, because great is your reward in heaven?

What? Are you kidding me?

When we look at the reality of our desperate state and of God, Himself, through the distorted wisdom of man and our world view, we see our present reality as hopeless and God as foolish. Here is a sobering thought—with all the riches, with all the might, with all the power and with all the intellect and knowledge this world has to offer…It was all defeated by foolishness at the cross!

So where can you find someone truly wise, truly educated, truly intelligent in this day and age? Hasn't God exposed it all as pretentious nonsense? Since the world in all its fancy wisdom never had a clue when it came to knowing God, God in his wisdom took delight in using what the world considered dumb--preaching, of all things!--to bring those who trust him into the way of salvation. — 1 Corinthians 1:20, 21 (MSG)

So who is the fool?

Because so many of my own false assumptions led to wrong conclusions, God was showing me the importance of understanding that which is true and real versus that which I thought was true and real. Because I had been so puffed up in my own pride and paralyzed by fear throughout most of my life, I had become a hardened fool. God needed to get me to a place where I could become teachable and where I could begin to see through a different lens. Unfortunately, I had to become broken and allow satan to chew on me before I came to a place where the ground became fertile enough for God to work with me and reveal the truth.

Ideas and images are the primary focus of Satan's efforts to defeat God's purposes for humankind. —Dallas Willard

Here is the truth. God is a redemptive and loving God who takes the initiative to reach out to us; He pursues us. We are the ones who so desperately need Him, but we have gone and made the world our friend. We are the ones, who should have been crying out for God to help us, but we don't and we continue living in our own selfish ways, not seeking or wanting Him, which echoes in every tear He cries.

He doesn't need us, but amazingly, He wants us. He wants to rescue us, to relate to us, to enjoy and delight and take pleasure in a personal relationship with us. So you know what He does? He trades Heaven for earth and enters our world to set things straight. The loving God of the universe became human, and lived here on earth among us in shared life and engaged us. Because God's human creation is made of flesh and blood, Jesus also became flesh and blood by being born in human form. For only as a human being could He die, and only by dying could He break the power of the devil and set things straight. He bled for everyone to set the captives free.

Don't you see?

Only the Son of the living God could defeat satan, so that God could be reconnected to all creation—to you—in a personal one-on-one relationship.

I have walked much of my life in fear, never truly finding a place where I knew I belonged. Rejection, victimization, and divorce has left me like a beggar, seeking desperately to find my blessing somewhere, to find it anywhere. I didn't know who I was or where I was going. I didn't know how significant I was or what the meaning of my life was, and the saddest part of this is that I didn't fully realize that God was holding the blessing for me that I was so desperately seeking.

So again I ask, "Who is the fool?"

This was the experience that the Lord used to shake loose the anchor that was so embedded into the false reality of all the lies that I somehow convinced myself was true. Each lie that I accepted as truth sent the anchor of my past deeper into my present reality and it was stuck. Divorce was not who I was; it was an awful event in my life that happened. It's not my identity!

I loosened my anchor!

Over time, I began to observe an amazing thing happen; the ripple effects of my journey and trials began to have an impact on others. At the time, I was living in a little apartment at the top of a barn in New Hampshire, and it was a weekend during which I had the kids. We came in after spending time exploring the woods that surrounded the barn, mostly because I had stepped in dark, stinky mud right up to my ankle. The kind of mud where you pull your leg out and your shoe is missing. The kids still remember and laugh at this.

After returning from our adventures in the woods, we ate and spent some time sitting around the table talking about the events of the day when out of the blue, my son made the comment, "Danae was right; you have changed Daddy." The Spirit of God used those penetrating words to open up a conversation that led my son and daughter into making a decision to let the Lord invade their precious little hearts. Placing their hearts in the tender caring hands of the Lord was a big first step. That day He began the process of wiping the tears from their faces.

During this season, the Lord began to renew and restore my relationships with my immediate family and many others. Also during this season, the Lord began revealing to me people to whom I needed to face, confess my wrongdoings, and ask for their forgiveness. I found that this was both a necessary and an extremely difficult process. The most difficult was my ex-wife and a new man in her life.

Collision

Two very important words: forgiveness and bitterness. Without the first you will limp through life with the second…Forgiveness must occur if you ever hope to be free of your painful past. It does not mean you agree. It doesn't necessarily mean you now have a close relationship with your offender. But it does mean you let it go…forever.
—Charles Swindoll

I was driving to my old house to pick up the kids for the weekend when the Lord brought into perspective a reality that I was intentionally running from for some time now—approaching my ex-wife to offer forgiveness and to ask for forgiveness. C. S. Lewis once said, "Everyone says forgiveness is a lovely idea until they have something to forgive." Walking to the door was like an eternity.

"This is not possible," I thought.

I was right, but somehow the Spirit of God provided me with the courage and the words to have the conversation with her. It didn't change the reality of the circumstances, but it was a scene painted with many questions and tears. A bit puzzled, she looked at me, but I just looked to the heavens and smiled.

A month later when I was picking up the kids and was still in the process of God, He wanted me to have a similar conversation with the new man in her life and offer forgiveness for him too.

"Yeah…right! You have got to be kidding me…there is no way!"

Honestly…I wanted to punch him right in the face.

"Lord…hell would have to freeze over before I will do that!"

God had a little chat with Jonah about going to the city of Nineveh and asked him to stand before them and speak a word of "offered" forgiveness. Jonah thought about that for a moment; said, "Yeah…right! You have got to be kidding me…there is no way"; and ran as far as he could in the opposite direction.

Do you know why that was?

Jonah was not very warmhearted toward the Ninevites, because they were in constant opposition with the Israelites—there was a collision. So when God told Jonah to go to these people, Jonah said, "No way God…You always forgive people and if I go to them, they may repent and You are going to forgive them, and I don't want that to happen! I want You to judge them!"

I could relate to Jonah, because I was not warmhearted toward this man, but hell did not freeze over, and that day I found myself standing at the door confronting this guy with an "offering" of forgiveness. This was one of the most difficult things I ever had to do. God brought me to this moment so He could see what was truly in my heart.

Imagine you find yourself in a prison-like setting. As you look around, you see a number of cells visible from where you're standing. You see people from your past incarcerated there—people who wounded you as a child. You see people you once called friends but who wronged you at some point in life. You might see one or both of your parents there, perhaps a brother or sister or some other family member. Even your spouse is locked in nearby, trapped with all the others in this jail of your own making.

This prison, you see, is a room in your own heart. This dark, drafty, depressing chamber exists inside you every day. But not far away, Jesus is standing there, extending you a key that will release every inmate.

No. You don't want any part of it. These people have hurt you too badly. They knew what they were doing and yet they did it anyway—even your spouse, the one you should have been able to count on most of all. So you resist and turn away. You're unwilling to stay any longer—seeing Jesus, seeing the key in His hand, knowing what He's asking you to do. It's just too much.

But trying to escape, you make a startling discovery. There is no way out. You're trapped inside with all the other captives. Your unforgiveness, anger, and bitterness have made a prisoner of you as well…Your freedom is now dependant on your forgiveness.[x]

These moments actually became my place of forgiveness, where love and hate collided!

As long as we are on earth, the love that unites us will bring us suffering by our very contact with one another, because this love is the resetting of a body of broken bones. Even saints cannot live with saints on this earth without some anguish, without some pain at the differences that come between them. There are two things [people] can do about the pain of disunion with other [people]. They can love or they can hate.[xi]

Not mind over matter, faith over circumstances—it must have taken a legion of angels to get me to that door. Asking for forgiveness and exposing our sins may be very difficult to do, but it is vital. The Lord loves each of us in spite of our sinful nature, but He loves us too much to leave us drowning in the muck and mire of our sins. God will do what is necessary to bring us into direct confrontation with our sins. This plays out throughout the pages of the bible. For example, God used the prophet Nathan to confront King David after he committed adultery with Bathsheba and attempted to cover it up by having her husband, Uriah, killed in battle.

The cross becomes our place of violent confrontation with our sins.

David came before the Lord and confessed these sins and God in His awesome grace and mercy forgave Him, but reminded him that there would still be consequences to these sins. God's forgiveness restores the broken relationship between Himself and us, but forgiveness doesn't make everything exactly as it was before. The sins we commit out of our own choices, whether we want to admit them or not, have a ripple effect and consequence that forgiveness cannot erase. It's like throwing a ball as hard as you can against a wall and it comes back and smacks you right in the face. The first thing we do is redirect blame. Stop concealing your sins, which God can see anyway, and stop blaming God for the choices you have made by exercising your own free will. Even though things may not be as they were before, confess what you have done before the Lord, come to Him in true and sincere repentance and He will forgive you. He will not bless an unrighteous life, but He desperately wants to bless a humble and repentant heart.

It's His nature to forgive!

When we begin to see people as God does, it becomes more difficult to view them as enemies. Forgiveness can be very painful, it may never make sense, and reconciliation may never happen. Whether you choose to forgive or not, you will still feel pain. I am learning that when I choose to forgive, it allows healing to takes place, which sets us free. The Greek word for forgiveness is aphiemi, and it means 'to let go, give up a debt, forgive, to remit, keep no longer.' It doesn't negate what the person did to you, but it does let them go free regardless of the offense. Forgiveness has little to do with what was done to us, but everything to do with what we choose to do with it. It's an act of grace; a gift from God that releases freedom and life. Although this was just the beginning on a long road to full forgiveness, my heart was willing and the choice was mine—I took the first step and it wasn't easy.

It must become our nature to forgive!

> If our actions or attitudes have brought hurt to another person there may be a need to go to that person and make right any wrong to break the destructive patterns in our relationships. God has forgiven us for the wrong the first time we ask. But to break the cycle of reaping from what we have sown and to begin restoring trust it is often necessary to make every effort to bring healing to others and to seek to restore the fractured relationship. Even if we feel the other person is 98% wrong and we are only 2% wrong, we are 100% responsible to walk in forgiveness and repentance for our 2%. (see Matthew 5:22–26; Psalm 109:17–19, 29).[xii]

His divine power has given us everything we need for life and godliness through our knowledge of Him who called us by his own glory and goodness. Through these he has given us his very great and precious promises, so that through them you may participate in the divine nature and escape the corruption in the world caused by evil desires. For this very reason, make every effort to add to your faith goodness; and to goodness, knowledge. —2 Peter 1:3–5 (NIV)

This is deeply rooted in the work of God's Spirit with regard to our sinful nature. He gives us a new nature, a holy nature. Also, for those of us who need more direction He gives a blueprint or a step plan toward wellness and health…here it is:

If my people, who are called by my name, will humble themselves and pray and seek my face and turn from their wicked ways, then will I hear from heaven and will forgive their sin and will heal their land. —2 Chronicles 7:14 (NIV)

Bethesda

I remember the words my sister shared with me as the reality of my divorce continued to paralyze me: "When that divorce letter was being written, the devil was laughing; when the divorce letter was delivered, all of hell rejoiced; but the story is not over." As the devil was strategizing on how to keep me paralyzed, he did not anticipate that I would invite Jesus into the desperate misery of my circumstances. There were countless days where I would lay paralyzed on my bed staring at the ceiling desperately wanting healing, so I could get up and walk against the riptide of my past.

In the Gospel of John, we read that Jesus comes across a paralytic man who has been in this place of affliction for thirty-eight years. When Jesus saw him lying there and learned that he had been in this condition for a long time, He asks this man the most important question of his life, **"Do you want to get well?"** The paralytic replied, "I have no one to help me into the pool when the water is stirred. While I am trying to get in, someone else goes down ahead of me." The biblical account of the Pool of Bethesda tells us that an angel would go down at a certain time into the pool and stir up the water and whoever stepped in first, after the stirring of the water, was made well of whatever disease they had.

The Lord continued to reveal Himself to me through His word, through my devotionals, through others and even in my dreams, but when He oriented my attention to this story, I began to realize one overwhelming resounding theme He was speaking to my heart: **"Rise Up!"** The same words He spoke to the man at the pool of Bethesda; then Jesus said to him, **"Rise [up!], pick up your bed and walk."** In that very moment, this man was healed, and he picked up his bed and walked.

There is significance to what was taking place here at this pool. After Jesus speaks these words to the paralytic man, He then commands the man to take up his bed and walk. He is essentially telling this man to get up and that there will be no turning back. So many of us take the first step of getting up on our feet when Jesus raises us up, but we make the mistake of continuing to carry the beds of our past and we never break free. Life continues; circumstances come against us; and we put down our bed again, lay down on it, and slip back into a paralytic state.

Jesus is telling us to get up and let it go!

What is wrong with us? For some reason we choose to journey through life on our own, without the Lord, and bounce from one sin or train wreck to another looking for that escape from the turbulence of life. Maybe this turbulence involves a relationship, a divorce, an affair, loss of a child, pride, lust, nonforgiveness or even religion; maybe its alcoholism, a drug addiction, depression, an eating disorder, or a chronic illness where a cure seems hopeless. Whatever is at the center of your turbulence, be assured you are not alone. We must come to an understanding that no matter how desperate our circumstances are we can find our answers and our hope in Jesus. Jesus healed the paralytic despite his obvious doubt and despite the fact that he didn't even know who Jesus was. I don't know what you are going through or why. I don't know the plans God has for you, but reach out to Him.

As I began to "rise up," I was not instantly made well, and I did not immediately let go of my past. I would still hold on to it like some sort of twisted security blanket that I thought would protect me from the fears that still consumed and crippled me—a learned response. So over many months, I would come before the Lord in prayer desperately wanting to be healed, desperately wanting to have the strength to walk away from my past into the freedom of the future. Then in God's perfect timing a breakthrough came, but the answer I received was not what I had expected. Experiencing more freedom through His grace and peace, He invited me to open up, to be more transparent, and to share my struggles with others.

Easier said than done!

Here are a few nuggets I picked up along the way.
- Before God can use you, you must develop a trusting relationship with Him and begin to see yourself through His eyes. Often times, it takes a crisis to

get you to this place and God will not hesitate to allow it, because He loves you. (sobering thought)
- Your testimony will become a mosaic of your deepest hurts. The stuff you're uncomfortable about, ashamed of, or don't want to share with others are exactly what God will use most to impact others.
- When you open up and reveal your failures, feelings and fears, there is a huge risk of rejection, but the benefits far outweigh the risks.

Failure is not fatal but failure to change might be. —John Wooden

I love the Message translation of Romans 8:1: *"With the arrival of Jesus, the Messiah, that fateful dilemma is resolved. Those who enter into Christ's being-here-for-us no longer have to live under a continuous, low-lying black cloud."* The paradox is that vulnerability is emotionally liberating, because opening up relieves stress and diffuses fears. This would become a big step to walking in more freedom and having major trust issues— I was scared!

When I mustered up enough courage to try walking with some transparency; opening up to my children, my family, my friends, my colleagues and many others the strangest thing happened…it blew them away! They had no idea of the extent of my brokenness and of how shattered my inner-self had become. They only saw what the world saw, my exterior: success, financial stability, and all the material possessions I surrounded myself with. I was still scared, but with this newfound transparency, I would begin to share details of my life with a courageous freedom, exposing the truth behind the person that everyone believed me to be. Walking in vulnerability created a safe place for others to begin to share their places of pain and struggle without fear of shame. This becomes a defining moment of impact when satan begins to lose hold of the darkness within us and the grip he has on our lives.

Those who get wet get healed when the waters are stirred!

In 2004 the Lord encouraged me to experience Promise Keepers, an event that brought clarity to many of the questions I needed answers to. This event also further exposed that I was a man in desperate need of a Savior. The Lord used a pastor in our group to give me the words of encouragement I needed to get up from that curb, wipe the tears from my face, and get back in the game.

Like the man at the pool of Bethesda…

I got up and walked it out.

The theme of Promise Keepers that year was "Uprising: The Revolution of a Man's Soul," which really connected with me because it brought more clarity to the words "rise up". The words the Lord spoke to my heart as a stepping stone to this event. The Promise Keepers experience was awesome, but a significant takeaway I heard at the event that resonates still to this day: "the things we fear actually determine the boundaries of our freedom." When all that we fear is God [reverence and awe], than the sum of all our fears become completely consumed in His love. It is written that perfect love casts away all fear! Don't beat yourself up if you haven't conquered all of your fears. I haven't—I'm still in the process.

> Give me a hundred men who love nothing but God and hate nothing but sin, and I will shake the whole world for Christ. —John Wesley

When we surrender our brokenness to the Lord, He will redeem it, and through this process, the tactics of the enemy of pulling someone down will ultimately raise them up! What hell intended for my defeat, God was able to use to bring redemption and victory. This is true; check out Romans 8:28.

Still

Can you remember a time in your life when you acted impulsively and later came to regret it? Maybe you impulsively ran out and bought a new car after being convinced from a TV commercial that it was exactly what you needed and soon regretted that decision because you really couldn't make the payments. Maybe it was the mortgage you signed without reading it carefully because you needed to have that new mansion of a house with a swimming pool, a golf-course lawn, and all the furnishings to maintain your image—just to realize that you are now a slave to it. Maybe it was that new job you took because it paid more, but later you discovered the reality that the grass isn't always greener on the other side. Whatever the decision may have been, you regretted it later.

Not that I always get it right, but I began learning the important lesson of God's perfect timing and the importance of waiting on Him. The Bible makes this vividly clear in Ecclesiastes 3:1 says, *"To everything there is a season, and a time to every purpose under the heaven" (KJV)*.

In the months following Promise Keepers, the Lord moved me into a season of learning the importance of being still and waiting upon Him. This was not a time of inactivity, but a time when I was learning how to rest in Him through the circumstances that came my way. These were extremely difficult, lonely, and necessary lessons to learn for my growth. It was not my nature to be still, to wait, and to remain idle; I kept hammering at God with absolutely no answer! I continued crying out to God, waiting for Him to show up on the scene and fix things, but nothing happened, and I became more and more frustrated. Needing Him every day, I would ask Him where He had gone. It was like a scene from a long family road trip with the kids in the back of the vehicle incessantly saying, "Are we there yet?" and the parents finally uttering a simple "No."

After some time the Lord would answer me by directing me to Psalms 46:10a, *"Be still, and know that I am God."* Not particularly liking this response, I continued to grumble, so God used an e-mail from my cousin to get His point across in a different way. The e-mail had a poem called "Wait" attached to it; check it out.

Wait

Desperately, helplessly, longingly, I cried,
Quietly, patiently, lovingly God replied.
I pled and I wept for a clue to my fate,
And the Master so gently said, "Child, you must wait."

"Wait? You say, wait!" my indignant reply.
"Lord, I need answers, I need to know why!
Is your hand shortened? Or have you not heard?
By Faith, I have asked, and am claiming your word.

My future and all to which I can relate
Hangs in the balance and YOU tell me to WAIT?
I'm needing a "yes'," a go-ahead sign,
Or even a "no" to which I can resign.

And Lord, You promised that if we believe
We need but to ask, and we shall receive.
And Lord, I've been asking, and this is my cry:
I'm weary of asking! I need a reply!

Then quietly, softly, I learned of my fate
As my Master replied once again, "You must wait."
So, I slumped in my chair, defeated and taut
And grumbled to God, "So, I'm waiting ... for what?"

He seemed, then, to kneel, and His eyes wept with mine,
And he tenderly said, "I could give you a sign.
I could shake the heavens, and darken the sun.
I could raise the dead, and cause mountains to run.

All you seek, I could give, and pleased you would be.
You would have what you want—But, you wouldn't know Me.
You'd not know the depth of My love for each saint;
You'd not know the power that I give to the faint.

You'd not learn to see through the clouds of despair;
You'd not learn to trust just by knowing I'm there;
You'd not know the joy of resting in Me
When darkness and silence were all you could see.

You'd never experience that fullness of love
As the peace of My Spirit descends like a dove;

> You'd know that I give and I save…(for a start),
> But you'd not know the depth of the beat of My heart.
>
> The glow of My comfort late into the night,
> The faith that I give when you walk without sight,
> The depth that's beyond getting just what you asked
> Of an infinite God, who makes what you have LAST.
>
> You'd never know, should your pain quickly flee,
> What it means that "My grace is sufficient for Thee."
> Yes, your dreams for your loved one overnight would come true,
> But, Oh, the Loss! If I lost what I'm doing in you!
>
> So, be silent, My Child, and in time you will see
> That the greatest of gifts is to get to know Me.
> And though oft may My answers seem terribly late,
> My most precious answer of all is still, "WAIT."
>
> —Russell Kelfer[xiii]

Still not fully grasping what He was trying to teach me and still not wanting to wait around for something to happen, I would continue to act independently of the Lord's timing which always seemed to make matters worse. Waiting is difficult, but God always has a purpose in all of His delays.

Repeating this pattern again and again with similar results, I started to discover what He was trying to teach me. I came to the realization that it was ridiculous to think that I could outmaneuver God; so I started learning to hand over the reins of striving in my own strength and began to wait upon the Lord. I didn't like it, but I did it. Not running headlong into your circumstances and waiting on the Lord requires courage not to lose hope or to lose heart. It's hard to stand in God's will, being quiet, calm and confident while your circumstances swirl around you.

"Watch and wait for his leading." —Samuel Dickey Gordon

I later understood that these seasons of silence were times of teaching, not periods of God's displeasure with me. It was important to just wait upon God and be completely grounded in Him.

Surrender

How far do we have to go to find our place of surrender in Him?

Arriving at the place where I was ready to begin surrendering more areas of my life to Him turned out to be a difficult process because even though all this stuff held me in bondage, it was all I had ever known. I was in such a relationship with my brokenness—I became co-dependent on it.

My identity was with my crisis not with my Christ.

He was inviting me to surrender my job, my finances, my circumstances, my children, and my life—everything to Him. It was at this place of surrender where people around me would spew out venom in my face with a vicious ferocity. It was at this place of surrender where people would find joy in tearing me down, and I would further feel the deep, cutting sting of rejection. It was at this place of surrender where I would have to make the painful walk down the Via Dolorosa, or Way of the Cross, from my judgment to my place of crucifixion.

It was time to run up that hill with the One who gave it all!

Up that hill to where the crimson river flows.

I discovered that these very people had nailed me to my cross where I became crucified with Him. Every part of me wanted to come off the cross and lash out at them, but my hands were affixed. I was weakened and incapacitated; my hands were nailed to the cross, and I had no choice but to endure the pain. The pain and the humiliation were unbearable, but He gave me the strength to persevere, to bless my adversaries, and to make them the very paving stones to my divine oneness with the Lord. I found that the cross is the place where joy and sorrow meet. It's a place where we realize that He alone is God and we surrender to His ways!

It's a place where He gives grace to the accused and condemned!

It's the place where He gives us life again!

When we are lowered into the water, it is like the burial of Jesus; when we are raised up out of the water, it is like the resurrection of Jesus. Each of us is raised into a light-filled world by our Father so that we can see where we're going in our new grace-sovereign country. Could it be any clearer? Our old way of life was nailed to the Cross with Christ, a decisive end to that sin-miserable life--no longer at sin's every beck and call! What we believe is this: If we get included in Christ's sin-conquering death, we also get included in his life-saving resurrection. We know that when Jesus was raised from the dead it was a signal of the end of death-as-the-end. Never again will death have the last word. When Jesus died, he took sin down with him, but alive he brings God down to us. From now on, think of it this way: Sin speaks a dead language that means nothing to you; God speaks your mother tongue, and you hang on every word. You are dead to sin and alive to God. That's what Jesus did.
—Romans 6:4–11 (MSG)

Into the tomb I was carried…

Please don't run out and hang yourself on a cross, because that would really hurt. I am purely painting a metaphor to describe the process of dying to ourselves and being resurrected with Jesus.

I desperately searched for a warm embrace throughout my childhood, but somehow I ended up chasing the wrong things—coming up empty, which left me with many areas of unmet needs and love deficits. I remembered all the nights when, as a child, I would sit at the bottom of the stairs sick, scared, or just wanting a hug. I would debate myself with a crippling agony for hours rationalizing which was easier—sitting on my bottom step alone and dealing with it or waking my mom up, knowing what her response would be. My dad wasn't present, because he was always working. My mom was there, but wasn't always present. My parents were not physically divorced, but it really felt like they were emotionally divorced. I just wanted a hug—a warm embrace. Unfortunately, I would usually make the choice of sitting there alone in isolation, which set the stage for how I would deal with circumstances throughout my life.

It took me quite some time to connect the dots that my Heavenly Father was waiting for me to surrender these places into His outstretched hands so He could come and fill them with an outpouring of His love. Identifying with this learned isolation, I would take it upon myself to fill my needs and deficits with all kinds of counterfeit affections, not realizing what I was really looking for could only be found in Him. It would take years to understand this pattern and to come to a place of letting go and of forgiving my parents. God helped me understand that they couldn't give away what they had never received.

>We were not created to journey through life with brokenness and emptiness.

>This was not how it was supposed to be.

>Until you taste God's love, the sense of emptiness cannot be satisfied.

God loves us so much that He wants to destroy all the things in our lives that keep us from living in relationship with Him, but somehow we choose to turn our eyes away from the Lord and focus on the things of this world. We see others having a good time, and convince ourselves that we are not. Here is a hard lesson that I learned—it might look like others are having fun today, but sooner or later, there will be a price to pay.

>We will reap what we sow!

You will not regret living your life for Jesus, because you will never find complete joy or fulfillment through relationships, success, possessions, or accomplishments outside of Him. You will only find the joy and fulfillment you are looking for in life through a relationship with Jesus Christ!

Among those who belong to Christ, everything connected with getting our own way and mindlessly responding to what everyone else calls necessities is killed off for good—crucified. —Galatians 5:24 (MSG)

We must allow the Lord to take us through this process because it is only through this process that we are resurrected with Him and we can begin to walk in newness of life. As I continued to find rest at that place of surrender, He would draw near to me, lift me up, and embrace me within His comforting arms, keeping me still; He would meet me at my place of need. Without a care in the world, I would just rest in the arms of my Abba, my Daddy God.

> If you want to be a true follower of Jesus, you need to take up your cross. "Then said Jesus unto his disciples, If any man will come after me, let him deny himself, and take up his cross, and follow me" (Matthew 16:24). That may sound miserable to some of us. You envision yourself carrying around some huge, wooden cross—living a miserable life, a life of selfless sacrifice. Let me share something with you. Taking up the cross of Christ means that I come to the Lord and say, "God, I realize you know more about life than I do. You know my future and what is best for me. And Lord, I want what You want for me more than what I want for myself. I am willing to put Your will above my own. If that means letting go of something that would hold me back or hurt me spiritually, I'm willing. If that means cutting loose something that is dragging me down, I'm willing. Because I know that You love me and have my best interest in mind." That is why the Apostle Paul said, "I am crucified with Christ: nevertheless I live; yet not I, but Christ liveth in me: and the life which I now live in the flesh I live by the faith of the Son of God, who loved me, and gave himself for me." (Galatians 2:20). The greatest life is the life that has been exchanged—the life that has been given to God. And the greatest life is living in obedience to Jesus Christ.[xiv]

I began to set my compass "due Jesus" and focused more on Him instead of the waves and the storms that surrounded me. As I began to place more of my identity in the Lord, the world around me began to just fade away and He provided me the strength to lay aside the stuff that entangled me. Remember, Jesus does not back away from the hard stuff in our lives!

It has been said that you can't direct the wind, but you can adjust your sails. I cannot control the world. I would love to if I could. Nor can I control the circumstances that come my way. But I can control my reaction to them. I can redirect my sails and adapt. We all will face storms, difficulties, and even shipwrecks. So it is time for us to develop our sea legs and not focus so much on how to avoid storms, but on how to get through them, how to survive them, and how to learn the lessons that we can only learn in such places.[xv]

We are pressed on every side by troubles, but we are not crushed. We are perplexed, but not driven to despair. We are hunted down, but never abandoned by God. We get knocked down, but we are not destroyed. —2 Corinthians 4:8–9 (NLT)

I wanted to stay the course and not deviate.

Strength

In the wilderness, you will begin to see the hand of God transforming your life when your faith stays laser focused on Him, even though the circumstances and storms of life chaotically swirl around you. When we open our hearts to the living God, He will begin to supernaturally transform you from the inside out as you become more like Him. In this process of being molded and shaped, you will find it easier to not allow the storms and circumstances of life to knock you down and keep you down.

> God does not give us overcoming life—He gives us life as we overcome. The strain of life is what builds our strength. If there is no strain, there will be no strength. —Oswald Chambers

I believe that God will allow us to get to the end of ourselves and our resources so that we will finally stop fighting and panicking and just reach out to Him. An amazing thing happens when we finally come to our place of surrender through the process of becoming broken—we find strength!

As you immerse yourself in His story, you will see that in order for the Lord to use us to our fullest, we must be broken so we can be given a new kind of strength that is supernatural in origin. When we are broken, we will see with more clarity the weakness of human strength and come to the realization that we can do nothing in our own strength.

Behold, I go forward, but he is not there; and backward, but I cannot perceive him: On the left hand, where he doth work, but I cannot behold him: he hideth himself on the right hand, that I cannot see him: But he knoweth the way that I take: when he hath tried me, I shall come forth as gold. —Job 23:8–10 (KJV)

When He leads you into the wilderness, you will be confronted with a heart-wrenching deafening silence and a deep longing to hear God's comforting voice. In the wilderness, God will only provide what you need to survive. It may not be the filet mignon you desire or the brand-new sports car you want, but He will provide you with your daily bread, which may be exactly what you need. When you find yourself in this place, my simple words of encouragement to you are, welcome to the wilderness! At this point it may be tempting to substitute this book for a new log in your fireplace. But before you do, listen to these words from Os Hillman.

> If you have an important message to convey to someone, what is the best means of getting the message through? Have you ever tried to talk with someone who was so busy you could not get him to hear you? Distractions prevent us from giving our undivided attention to the messenger. So too, God has His way of taking us aside to get our undivided attention. For Paul, it was Arabia for three years; for Moses, it was 40 years in the desert; for Joseph, it was 13 years in Egypt; for David, it was many years of fleeing from King Saul. God knows the stubborn human heart. He knows that if He is to accomplish His deepest work, He must take us into the desert in order to give us the privilege to be used in His Kingdom. In the desert, God changes us and removes things that hinder us. He forces us to draw deep upon His grace. The desert is only a season in our life. When He has accomplished what He wants in our lives in the desert, He will bring us out. He has given us a mission to fulfill that can only be fulfilled after we have spent adequate time in preparation in the desert. Fear not the desert, for it is here you will hear God's voice like never before. It is here you become His bride. It is here you will have the idols of your life removed. It is here you begin to experience the reality of a living God like never before. Someone once said, "God uses enlarged trials to produce enlarged saints so He can put them in enlarged places!"[xvi]

Understanding what He is trying to teach us in the wilderness will become critical for spiritual survival. Remember that God's purpose in leading the Israelites into the wilderness was to teach and train them, but instead they saw it as punishment and they often grumbled. What God intended to be a brief time in the wilderness, the Israelites made a lifetime experience. Learn from this and as difficult as it is, let go and let God. For once we have spent sufficient time in the wilderness, He will draw us out.

Jesus is waiting for us to just surrender to Him!

Fourth Stone § Promised Land

"Don't be afraid, I've redeemed you. I've called your name. You're mine. When you're in over your head, I'll be there with you. When you're in rough waters, you will not go down. When you're between a rock and a hard place, it won't be a dead end—Because I am GOD, your personal God, The Holy of Israel, your Savior. I paid a huge price for you…That's how much you mean to me! That's how much I love you! I'd sell off the whole world to get you back, trade the creation just for you.

Isaiah 43:1–4 (MSG)

This is the land of sin and death and tears…but up yonder is unceasing joy! —D. L. Moody

Signposts

That's right. Because I, your GOD, have a firm grip on you and I'm not letting go. I'm telling you, "Don't panic. I'm right here to help you." —Isaiah 41:13 (MSG)

The Lord picked me up and carried me out of the Egypt that I had created from my freedom of choice. He helped me cross the Red Sea, protected me from my enemies, and led me out into the wilderness where I would spend lots of time with Him. I found it amazing that the Lord was bringing me on my own journey to the Promised Land as He did the Israelites, but I would still need to face many obstacles and battles.

The first one was my river Jordan experience, and it stood before me!

That the waters which came down from above stood and rose up upon a heap very far from the city Adam, that is beside Zaretan: and those that came down toward the sea of the plain, even the salt sea, failed, and were cut off: and the people passed over right against Jericho. —Joshua 3:16 (KJV)

I find the circumstances and details of my life's journey juxtaposed within the pages of Joshua chapter four, when after crossing the river Jordan the Israelites renewed their commitment to God. The crossing of the river Jordan was symbolic of God moving His people from the wilderness into the Promised Land, a place of transition. The miraculous crossing of the Red Sea forty years earlier represented the deliverance of God's people from the bondage in Egypt. After that incredible miracle, God's people were now set free to proceed toward the Promised Land, but once they were freed from their place of bondage, they had too little faith and too much fear to cross the Jordan River and possess the land God had offered them. Opportunity was before the Israelites because after decades of God working with them in the wilderness, after strengthening their faith and obedience, they were now willing and ready to enter and, by God's strength, defeat all obstacles to victory and rest in the land.

Here is what's interesting about this area: after Jacob crossed the Jabbok River on his way back to Israel, after leaving Harran, he found himself in a wrestling match with the angel of the Lord (or perhaps God Himself), at which point he was given a new name. The Jabbok River leads west into the Sukkot Valley, from where one would cross over the Jordan and could easily reach Shechem, as Jacob eventually did. The biblical cities of Zaretan and Adam are also at the mouth of the valley.

This place, this intersection of two streams, was where there was a conflict between two paths. Just like my crossroads. Was I ready to be led out of my wilderness experience to seize the inheritance of my Promised Land? Was I ready to get real with God and commit to Him?

This is where we, too, will wrestle with God, because we have to decide to move forward or turn back. What makes this decision difficult for us is that we may be able to achieve things in our own strength in the wilderness, but it's impossible without God's strength in the Promised Land. This is where we make that critical turning point—our way or God's way!

The people came up out of the Jordan on the tenth day of the first month. They set up camp at The Gilgal (The Circle) to the east of Jericho. Joshua erected a monument at The Gilgal, using the twelve stones that they had taken from the Jordan. And then he told the People of Israel, "In the days to come, when your children ask their fathers, 'What are these stones doing here?' tell your children this: 'Israel crossed over this Jordan on dry ground.' "Yes, GOD, your God, dried up the Jordan's waters for you until you had crossed, just as GOD, your God, did at the Red Sea, which had dried up before us until we had crossed. This was so that everybody on earth would recognize how strong GOD's rescuing hand is and so that you would hold GOD in solemn reverence always." —Joshua 4:19–24 (MSG)

Joshua and the people had just crossed the Jordan River. They were camped at Gilgal. But before they could proceed they were required to circumcise all the males, because a whole new generation had grown up while living in the desert. This is where Israel, like a worm in a cocoon, was transformed. Circumcision is bloody, personal, and it exposes all that you are. God was saying that before you can become His army, you must roll away the reproach of the Egyptian way of life. You are no longer a slave to the ways of Egypt. It is a time to put aside the old way of life. Many are walking around as goats in sheep's clothes, practicing a form of religion without the true source of truth and power. Sin in our midst testifies against us. It keeps us in Egypt and never allows us to enter the Promised Land. Our lives must be circumcised in order for us to come out of Egypt into our own Promised Land of spiritual blessing with God. This transformation marks the first time Israel begins to taste the fruit of the Promised Land. No more manna from Heaven. The manna stopped the day after they were circumcised. There was no longer any manna for the Israelites, but that year they ate produce from Canaan. …The cross of Jesus takes away all reproaches. Enter the Promised Land with power.[xvii]

The crossing of the river Jordan is the central theme here, but throughout the story, I invite you to discover that there is something many of us fail to see or simply overlook—stones. The end of the story is not the crossing of the river, but the pile of stones and their significance. The purpose of this "heap of stones" is to be a remembrance of the river crossing. There will be those who will make this journey at some point in their lives who have not experienced this great revelation of God; they will see the stones and ask about them. Then the story of God's great act for His people can be lived again through His telling. For me the stones in the story are not just stones or a "heap of stones" on the bank of a river; they became a marker that balanced my known past with my unknown future. They are a way to remember who the people are, who God is, and how we should be as God's people. The "heap of stones", my four stones, actually transcended the timeline of my past and became a symbol of hope, a guiding light that shone far beyond the banks of the Jordan, far beyond the time of Joshua, and intersected my life on my journey at the mountaintop.

One of these intersection points along my journey brought me to Edinburgh, Scotland, which at first glance was just another business trip. My time there was spent performing the necessary due diligence required to integrate and unify our global technology. However, Edinburgh Castle captured my thoughts as I could see its majestic structure rising upwards in the center of the city. In fact it would be hard to miss it. I have always had a fascination with castles, and I have had other opportunities to visit them throughout the United Kingdom, but there was a mysterious force drawing me to this particular castle.

We had worked hard all week and finished our work early, leaving Sunday open for exploring this magnificent city, so of course we headed right up to the castle. I believe that this was another God stumble, for what I found hidden in the middle of this awesome structure was a treasure of Scotland: the Stone of Destiny. I don't know about you, but thought this was really cool, although the guard didn't think so when I tried to get a picture of it.

In 1296 the Stone was captured by Edward I as spoils of war and taken to Westminster Abbey, where it was fitted into a wooden chair, known as St. Edward's Chair. On this chair, subsequent English sovereigns, except Queen Mary II, have been crowned. In 1996, the British Government decided that the Stone should be kept in Scotland when not in use at coronations, and on November 15, 1996, after a handover ceremony at the border between representatives of the Home Office and of the Scottish Office, it was returned to Scotland and transported to Edinburgh Castle where it remains today. Scottish tradition holds the Stone of Destiny to be the pillow stone said to have been used by the biblical Jacob.[xviii]

This in a sense became a signpost for me and I knew that woven into my business trip to a far away land was the confirmation of my destiny moment back on that mountain top. It's important to realize that this world is not our final destination; it is part of our journey! Many obstacles and sinful desires are at war with us in this life, and they usually are successful in distracting us from our goal and over time slowly erode our desire to complete our journey. It is only through the awesome sustaining power of the Spirit of God that we are given the confidence and character to journey through this world, trapped in darkness and so desperately needing God's light.

We desperately need these divine signposts to reorient us toward our goal!

These stones have become a signpost by which I can now stand in my present, look to my past, and then draw a straight line into my unknown future, which is already written by God Himself. They have become my compass, my destiny, which sets the means by which I can now define my present, and my future, by the way of my past. They are symbolic of the process of God.

All the mistakes and regrettable choices that I have made along my journey of life have placed an unbearable yoke of brokenness on me, but somehow He is leading me into the Promised Land and supernaturally making time wasted, useful again. I really thought that I had fallen out of His hands and lost His grace. I am really thankful that He is changing my perspective.

"Are you tired? Worn out? Burned out on religion? Come to me. Get away with me and you'll recover your life. I'll show you how to take a real rest. Walk with me and work with me—watch how I do it. Learn the unforced rhythms of grace. I won't lay anything heavy or ill-fitting on you. Keep company with me and you'll learn to live freely and lightly." —Matthew 28–30 (MSG)

With a broken compass and stumbling in the midst of life, I lost my direction and I couldn't see the beautiful picture that the Lord would one day complete in me. These stones, these signposts are evidence of the grace the Lord has left me, reminding me of everything I have been through and what it took for Him to get to me.

On to Jericho I had to go…

Strongholds

The enemy will not see you vanish into God's company without an effort to reclaim you. —C. S. Lewis

A stronghold is a powerfully fortified defensive structure, which because of its location, design, walls, and the capabilities of the armies that reside within it is hard to defeat. Armies that had the advantage and protection of a stronghold could launch attacks against anything that came against them, and then retreat to the safety of the walled city. This picture of a physical stronghold is comforting if the armies within it are good and are used to protect the land that is rightfully theirs. What if a stronghold was erected on your land by an invading army that was bent on your destruction? What if the stronghold is not supposed to be there, and no matter how many times you come up against it to tear down the walls, the armies within it crush you over and over again?

Throughout God's word, this picture of a physical stronghold is used to represent a spiritual stronghold. Spiritual strongholds are points of operation that our enemy uses where he wages the battle against us. Satan's goal is to defeat us and to prevent us from seeing the truth of God and how much God loves us.

> Do the strongholds of your Jericho that hide your pride, control, and addictions paralyze you in fear?

When a war is waged in the spiritual realm through these strongholds, the effects of the battle are connected to real events in our physical lives. For example, let's consider the journey of the Israelites from their place of bondage in Egypt to their place of freedom and redemption in the Promised Land. The scene becomes desperate for the Israelites as they see Pharaoh's army bearing down on them and they begin to panic because they don't believe God. It says in Exodus 14:11, they told Moses, *"Weren't the cemeteries large enough in Egypt so that you had to take us out here in the wilderness to die? What have you done to us, taking us out of Egypt?"* Moses receives a revelation from the Lord and tells the Israelites to not be afraid, to stand firm, and to watch God do His work of salvation. The people continued to panic out of unbelief and Moses begins to pray to God. God basically tells Moses to knock it off and to get moving! There is a time to pray, but sometimes one must simply act in obedience and move forward! God removed the obstacle to victory, but an act of obedience and faith on the part of the Israelites enabled them to push through to the Promised Land.

We see the Israelites, who because of their unbelief and lack of faith were not able to receive the promises of God and spent forty years wandering in the wilderness. Only when they believed God at His word could they enter into the joy and rest of the Promised Land, but the faithless generation was kept out. In the same way today, many of us fail to receive the blessings promised because we do not believe God is strong enough to overcome the strongholds in our life.

These strongholds in our lives are essentially fortresses of thoughts that control and influence our attitudes. They define or filter how we view certain situations, circumstances, and even the people around us. They become the lens we see through distorting our view. When we continue to come into agreement with these thoughts and activities, they can actually become habitual, and when this happens, we open ourselves up for a spiritual fortress to be built up in us. This happens at a subconscious level where the enemy launches his attack on the battlefield of our mind.

One of the major strongholds that satan used as a base of operation in my life was that of rejection, an arrow he shot into my heart in the womb. My perception of life and of God became twisted by these patterns of thought; I was always listening to the voice that told me, "Don't let them in; they will only hurt you." My mind was always going a mile a minute, always thinking, controlling, manipulating and keeping others and God from coming too close to my heart. I found ways to keep them away from my feelings and would continue to hide how much I was hurting. I simply didn't trust and didn't let people know me or allow them to get too close to me because I was afraid. I pushed everyone including God away. I didn't want to give anyone a chance to hurt me any further than I had already been hurt, so I didn't let anyone into my heart and my life to truly get to know me. That way, if they rejected me and never truly knew me, I could simply say that I didn't care. If I let myself care, it would just hurt more. I also believed the lie that if I let God into my heart, He would somehow use it against me or He would not like me. I was protecting myself at all cost even to the point of pushing those who loved me out of my life by rejecting them before they could reject me. I had an overwhelming fear of being vulnerable.

Because of this stronghold in my life, I believed the lie that I had to "perform" to be worthy of love and acceptance. This battle caused me to become more and more performance oriented, which alienated my affections from my Heavenly Father whose love for me was more than I could have ever imagined. This performance-driven life made me think money was the only way to have friends, power or value and at a very young age I was determined to gain wealth, so I could master the world around me. My entire existence became centered on money and power, making them my god and my idol. Only after my idol was crushed with my divorce did I begin to seek the truth out of desperation. Satan ruled over my life from this stronghold and, over time, my pursuit of what I thought was the road to love and acceptance. I became a bitter and angry person who also alienated those closest to me. This constant struggle to gain the love and acceptance of others paralyzed me in a life of task orientation and working to please someone rather than with an intimacy and relationship orientation that God had already freely offered me.

I didn't see or want to believe the truth!

There were other strongholds that the Lord had to bring down in my life (and I'm sure there are more), but some of the battles that were extremely tough to fight were the ones in which I could not see the enemy fighting against me. As I pursued Him in prayer to understand this more, the Lord began to slowly open my eyes to the intense realities of spiritual warfare and how deep the deception of the enemy was. He allowed me to see and experience things during my journeys that I would have not believed unless I saw them with my own eyes.

One of these battles began when overwhelming feelings of fear and anger wove together with threads of sadness, tightening its grip on me as I reflected upon my precious children. Through the tears, I found the courage to shout out with a battle cry to the enemy: "I have allowed you to take much from me, but as long as I stand I will defend my children!"

"Conviction is worthless until it converts itself into conduct." —Thomas Carlyle

In my selfish pursuit of obtaining wealth for my children's inheritance, I failed to see and understand that I was not leaving them a Godly inheritance, one that would last for eternity. I learned that it is our responsibility to leave our children with a legacy of Godly values, not just a material inheritance; but it is impossible to achieve this if we continue to spend all our time pouring ourselves into our careers and our pleasures. This is only completely secured by the priority we place upon our relationships with our children. The reality is that my divorce was a place of failure for their mom and me, because our kids didn't sign up for any of this. As a dad, I don't want my children to experience the pain that I experienced because of my stupid mistakes, I want better for them. I hope that these four stones will become markers in the lives of my children so they will remember my journey. The good news…the story isn't over.

Have you ever thought of your children being treasures worth fighting for?

There are times along our journey when God calls us to stand in the authority of His Son; to engage in spiritual warfare against the enemy of our souls and shout with authority, "Enough—thus far and no more!" This is not something we should take lightly, because there is not an earthly power that rivals that of satan, and whenever he wages war against one of God's children, he does so by trying to intimidate and paralyze us through fear. We need God to fight the battle.

In 1 Samuel, we read the awesome account of the confrontation of David and Goliath. The scene unfolds where David is asked by his father to bring some food down to the battle at Ephes-Dammin, which literally means "edge of blood." At this point in the story, Goliath has been relentlessly taunting the army of Israel for thirty-nine straight days, simply beating them down through intimidation and fear. David walks into the scene on the fortieth day as Goliath continues to curse and intimidate the army of Israel. This shepherd boy looks back at one of the soldiers and says, "Who does this guy think he is and what do I get for shutting this fool up?" David stands before this giant enemy of Israel, picks up five stones and with divine line of sight, sends a stone deep into the head of Goliath sending him to his death on the ground.

There are giants in our land that aren't supposed to be there!

Goliath's formidable size and arrogant boasting intimidated Israel's army, and because God's anointing had fallen from King Saul, he was unable to respond with courage to Goliath's charge of intimidation and paralyzing fear. God's anointing had fallen on David, who was just a young simple shepherd boy but was mighty in spirit. David did not tremble at the size or shouts of Goliath—he saw Goliath through God's eyes. David had righteous anger for the disrespect shown to the armies of the living God. David did not weigh the risk of failure because his faith was resting totally in God. Learning that these are merely the tactics of the enemy designed to instill fear will allow us to stand firm in God's power to overcome anything that comes against us.

I love the scene from J. R. R Tolkien's "The Return of the King" where Aragon is desperately outnumbered. He looks fear right in the eye and finds the strength to inspire his men against what seems like an almost certain defeat against the massive forces of the enemy. Standing firm and riding in front of his army, he declares,

I see in your eyes the same fear that would take the heart of me.
A day may come when the courage of men fails,
when we forsake our friends and break all bonds of fellowship,
...but it is not this day! This day we fight!
By all that you hold dear on this good earth,
I bid you stand...[xix]

Sounds so easy in the movies, doesn't it? Ambrose Redmoon defines courage as not having the absence of fear, but rather the judgment that something else is more important than fear. "God, I am afraid, but give me the courage to push through my fears, the burdens of a passive spirit and the regret of my past failures." It was time for me to take up the sword of the Spirit, the word of God and to go to war on behalf of righteousness; it was time to begin the battle for my children! All this stuff, the garbage that has burdened my life for so long and all the generational issues that had been passed down, had to end with me. I did not want any of this to be passed down to my children, and I asked the Lord to do whatever He needed to do in my life to free my children of these chains and burdens that I have carried for so long. Unfortunately, I had to walk through another failed marriage for me to really get this. To break free of old patterns, to stand up and become the man God called me to be.

As in the scenes of Jericho and David's battle with Goliath, it is only through the Lord's power that we will be able to be break free from satan's control. When we begin to allow God to invade our lives, His word will reveal the control that satan has in our lives through strongholds. We need to identify where these strongholds are and in the power and might of the Lord have them torn down and destroyed. An army first has to remove the strongholds, to conquer the land and we need to do the same in the strength of the Lord.

Waving the banner of the Lord before me, it was time to storm the encampment of the enemy and reclaim territory for Jesus Christ; it was time to storm my Jericho.

The Battle

To my selfish gain, living this life to satisfy my own
Blinded by the deception; so foolish, I believed the lies.
The foundation crumbles; my marriage, my family; dies!
Many tears I cry, living the lesson of reaping what I have sown.

A raging river of sorrow rushes through my broken heart.

The enemy has taken so much! These precious gifts, stolen away.
Too long in this slumber! Shaken, I awake; through the long night I pray.
Can't wait any longer! Whatever it takes; from You I can't be apart

A blessed revelation of Your divine Oneness!
With Your embrace, I leave my Hiding Place!
Giving me the strength to stand, You Cover Me!
A vision of my purpose now set! I fire the Four Stones!

Realizing these journeys I have walked, You have been right there by my side.

Heavenly Father, at Your feet I fall; I come now to Your throne!
Your purpose for my life now revealed. Your love I now embrace.
I freely give You my ALL until that day when I see Your face.
Take me higher; I am not afraid, I now know that I am not alone!

"I love you, GOD—you make me strong. GOD is bedrock under my feet, the castle in which I live, my rescuing knight. My God--the high crag where I run for dear life, hiding behind the boulders, safe in the granite hideout." —Psalm 18:1, 2 (MSG)

I make my declaration to the Lord God Almighty…

Here I am! I stand ready to give up my life for the One.
Here I am! I stand ready to pour out my heart for the Son.

All I want is to be faithful! All I want is You my Lord!
All I want is Your awesome love! Let it fall, let it burn within me!
With this love you have given me, let it set the world around me on fire!
To be a friend of the Almighty God is all I desire!

With the supernatural strength and power of my Lord Jesus Christ, I rise!

"For God hath not given us the spirit of fear; but of power, and of love, and of a sound mind." —2 Timothy 1:7 (KJV)

I accept the call of the Lord to stand! To rise up! To fight! He prepares me for the battle!

"And that about wraps it up. God is strong, and he wants you strong. So take everything the Master has set out for you, well-made weapons of the best materials. And put them to use so you will be able to stand up to everything the devil throws your way. This is no afternoon athletic contest that we'll walk away from and forget about in a couple of hours. This is for keeps, a life-or-death fight to the finish against the devil and all his angels. Be prepared. You're up against far more than you can handle on your own. Take all the help you can get, every weapon God has issued, so that when it's all over but the shouting you'll still be on your feet." —Ephesians 6:10–13 (MSG)

In the name of the Lord Jesus Christ I affirm the protection of the belt of truth. I fasten it securely around my waist!

I embrace the righteousness that is mine by faith in the Lord Jesus Christ. Affirming my victory, by His covering, I put on the breastplate of righteousness!

Accepting Your declaration that I am justified and that I have peace with you, by faith and in the Name of the Lord Jesus Christ I confidently put on the shoes of peace!

I rely on Your holy presence to surround me offering me total protection. Loving heavenly Father, I take by faith the protection of the shield of faith!

I am secure and I recognize that my salvation is the Person of Your Son, the Lord Jesus Christ. Covering my mind with Jesus, I take by faith the helmet of salvation and place it on my head!

I stand before my Lord with His armor securely on! With the Lion of Judah at my side, I am prepared to stand against the forces of darkness and advance the Kingdom of my precious Lord and Savior. The Almighty God!

Embracing its truth and awesome power; with my hand I firmly grasp and lay hold of the mighty sword of the Spirit, the word of God! With determination, I hold it high! With the Spirit of God guiding me into the truth of the word of God!

With the battle cry of the Lord, I charge into the fight!

In the name of the Lord Jesus Christ I accept my position of pulling down strongholds! With the love of the Lord firmly set within my heart, with the protection of His strength and power, I bring all the work of the Lord Jesus Christ directly against all the forces of darkness. I pray the victory of our Lord's incarnation, crucifixion, resurrection, ascension, and all of His glory against satan and his armies. By the authority given to me by the Lord Jesus Christ, I claim the promises of Your word and wield the sword strong against satan to defeat him, to strike him down, to reclaim the ground he has taken and to win great victories for my God!

"The world is unprincipled. It's dog-eat-dog out there! The world doesn't fight fair. But we don't live or fight our battles that way--never have and never will. The tools of our trade aren't for marketing or manipulation, but they are for demolishing that entire massively corrupt culture. We use our powerful God-tools for smashing warped philosophies, tearing down barriers erected against the truth of God, fitting every loose thought and emotion and impulse into the structure of life shaped by Christ. Our tools are ready at hand for clearing the ground of every obstruction and building lives of obedience into maturity. You stare and stare at the obvious, but you can't see the forest for the trees. If you're looking for a clear example of someone on Christ's side, why do you so quickly cut me out? Believe me, I am quite sure of my standing with Christ." —2 Corinthians 10:3–7 (MSG)

I rest in the presence of my Lord in a vast field of green, deeper than the color than that of any emerald, standing with the ones I love dearly. Angels filling the sky…surrounded by His grace, I gently feel the winds caress my smiling face of joy with His warm embrace.

The Lord Jesus in all of His power and glory rushes by on the most spectacular heavenly white horse one has ever seen! Whiter and purer than the gentle snow!

With the courage, the strength and the love now present in our spirits, my loved ones and I mount our white horses and without wavering join our Lord Jesus Christ as we race with Him over these fields of green with the warm gentle wind rushing through our hair. With an unbelievable joy, one of my loved ones looks back at me and cries out…Here we go!"

In that moment, with all the heavenly hosts around us; with a passion we jump through a rainbow into the clouds with our majestic Lord…

"And I saw heaven opened, and behold a white horse; and he that sat upon him was called Faithful and True, and in righteousness he doth judge and make war. His eyes were as a flame of fire, and on his head were many crowns; and he had a name written, that no man knew, but he himself. And he was clothed with a vesture dipped in blood: and his name is called The word of God. And the armies which were in heaven followed him upon white horses, clothed in fine linen, white and clean. And out of his mouth goeth a sharp sword, that with it he should smite the nations: and he shall rule them with a rod of iron: and he treadeth the winepress of the fierceness and wrath of Almighty God. And he hath on his vesture and on his thigh a name written, KING OF KINGS, AND LORD OF LORDS." —Revelation 19:11–16 (KJV)

He is coming to wage the battle!

Jump

As the Lord continued adjusting the lenses of my spiritual eyes to see the invisible more clearly, I began to understand that my battles were not with the people who I thought were bent on seeing my destruction—my battles were with the unseen forces of darkness.

We have one enemy and that is satan!

People are not our enemies!

It was time for me to refuse to be held in bondage as a victim of my circumstances and to rise up and declare the truth of His awesome and holy name! Once I received a revelation in this area, the Lord began to strengthen my armor and called me into deeper levels of prayer. In Ephesians 6:18 it is written, *"In the same way, prayer is essential in this ongoing warfare. Pray hard and long. Pray for your brothers and sisters. Keep your eyes open. Keep each other's spirits up so that no one falls behind or drops out."* (MSG) This milestone would become the place in my journey that I could actually begin to pray for people who continued to tear me down and this was not easy, but I have heard that it's tough to be angry with people you are praying for. Love does what is needed, it does what is necessary, and it is always serving and sacrificing for others just as our Lord and Savior Jesus Christ did for us.

Then will I sprinkle clean water upon you, and ye shall be clean: from all your filthiness, and from all your idols, will I cleanse you. A new heart also will I give you, and a new spirit will I put within you: and I will take away the stony heart out of your flesh, and I will give you a heart of flesh. And I will put my spirit within you, and cause you to walk in my statutes, and ye shall keep my judgments, and do them. And ye shall dwell in the land that I gave to your fathers; and ye shall be my people, and I will be your God. —Ezekiel 36:25–28 (MSG)

The trees were proudly parading their vivid colors that warm and inviting autumn day in October of 2003 as I headed out to Orange, Massachusetts, to jump out of a perfectly good airplane. Upon my arrival to the jump school, an employee with a detached personality and a large Mohawk haircut handed me a phonebook-size bundle of paperwork so I could begin the long process of signing my life away; so I wouldn't hold the jump school responsible if I ended up a human pancake.

If that wasn't enough, the whole family decided to show up to see if I would really follow through with this incredibly crazy stunt, which meant there was no way I could chicken out. You know, we men have our pride.

Anyway, I at least had enough sense to do a tandem jump, which meant that a professional jump instructor would be physically harnessed to my back for the exciting trip down. I spent the remainder of the day learning how to summon the courage to jump out of the plane and waiting for what seemed an eternity for my trip up to 13,500 feet.

My name was finally called and as I looked back at my family, possibly for the last time, I was led to the equipment area where the jump school staff helped me put on my jumpsuit, harness and a crazy-looking helmet that resembled something out of the 1940s football era. So there I was, fully geared up, standing with a silent numbness as my brain worked overtime to convince me not to do this, when out comes my assigned jump instructor.

You know—the professional.

This guy had a military-style crew cut, was half my size, was wearing no shoes, and was downing a can of Red Bull. His first words of encouragement to me were, "Dude, we are going to drop like a rock!" If that wasn't enough, to further convince me that I was doing the right thing, out comes the videographer and his nickname was Slick. I was jumping out of a plane with Dude and Slick!

We finished gearing up and began what seemed like an endless walk to the aircraft that sat motionless as it idled on the safety of the tarmac. The scene then slipped into slow motion as I watched my family waving to me while I walked toward the aircraft with a veiled confidence, knowing that I would need a change of underwear real soon. The trip up to altitude was the loudest, longest twenty minutes of my life, and that the jump instructor and videographer found amusement in ribbing me the entire ride didn't help.

The alarm sounds.

Altitude is 13,500 feet.

The door opens.

The wind comes roaring in.

Panic begins to overtake me.

Changed my underwear. (Just kidding.)

My test of courage had finally come as I began to inch my way toward the open door of my destiny moment. I stood at the threshold of all I knew to be safe, and without any rational thought, we leaped out of the plane, heading toward the ground at over 150 mph.

I am at the edge.

Stripped of everything, I made my wilderness jump.

As the events of that day began to fade into my pages of history, I imagined a conversation between the Lord and me to go something like this: **"Tim, help Me understand something here. You have no fear jumping out of an airplane with a complete stranger strapped to your back that you just met, half your size with a buzz cut, no shoes, and drinks Red Bull…but you won't let go of your fear and jump into your**

destiny that I have created you for? Tim jump for Me, and I will make you fearless!"

God has a unique perspective on our lives because He knows our story. The tough part is we don't have that perspective, and when He brings us into the wilderness, it can be terrifying. Because of our limited view, we focus on our circumstances while He focuses on using our circumstances to accomplish a deeper work in us. It's a trust issue. Can I trust God to shield me from the full onslaught of the enemy? Can I trust God when He allows suffering in my life? Can I trust God when He takes things away from me? Can I trust Him? Will I jump?

Confusion and fear were close companions in the wilderness, but I would later understand that God uses the wilderness experience to buff out the unseen lumps and cracks in us. In a sense, we become the pot on the Potter's wheel like in Jeremiah 18.

> There is a critical choice which confronts us in the wilderness times of our life. We can refuse to give up and boldly activate our faith and choose hope—or we can retreat into ourselves and become paralyzed in a dungeon of despair. —John Jewell

A starting point of understanding who He created us to be begins when we allow Him to step into the muck and mire of our lives. This place is where we need to find a way to surrender, give up control, and allow Him to do a deep work in us. So many of us are not being honest with ourselves, with our feelings, with our thoughts and with our actions, but God knows our heart. He wants to set us free.

He wants to unmask the imposter masquerading within us.

My eyes were opened to the difficult truth of how ignorant I was about myself. This ignorance fueled my fears, and overtime my faith became so self-centered that I created a God that existed to make my plans come true instead of His. I was conforming God to my plans creating the illusion of control. I was unable to see how much of a mess I was and I had to destroy the foolish idea that I had my life under control.

God continued to close me in until that destiny moment where He could get me alone with Himself. As long as my pride was in control of my choices and my life, He waited painfully at my side with tears in His eyes while I suffered through heartbreak and many other disappointments.

Do not misunderstand me here; my marriage was not what was hindering me. It was my hardened heart, selfish pride, and the many idols such as money, power, and status that I blindly chose to serve for so many years. What are the idols that you serve? Fill in the blank _____.

God knew my stubborn heart; He knows yours.

Winepress

In the wilderness, He reveals many areas of counterfeit affections and selfish desires, which sadly are part of so many of us. Many circumstances, habits, strongholds, and events in our lives that He will unravel in our wilderness journey are for most of us automatic responses or so habitual that we blindly slip into them.

For example, have you ever looked at your accomplishments as if you alone were the reason for your success? Have you ever thought your prosperity was due to your own ingenuity? Has your material success been a testimony to others that God is the ruler of all aspects of your life, even the material side of your life? Or do you even know who you are?

Out in the wilderness, these will be the very things He will use to get us alone with Him, and when He gets us alone, these become very clear. The only one who truly knows us and understands us is God! It's almost laughable to think that we know more about ourselves than the one who created us.

> If you yourself do not cut the lines that tie you to the dock, God will have to use a storm to sever them and to send you out to sea.—Oswald Chambers

The seasons of adversity that I had to endure actually allowed me to see and experience the awesome love and power of God as He revealed Himself through these difficult circumstances. In Matthew 14, we find the disciples right in the middle of a raging storm while out at sea. Jesus steps into this violent scene and approaches the boat by walking on the water like nothing's wrong, which actually freaked them out, as they thought they were seeing a ghost. Jesus, noticing their absolute fear and terror, says to them, **"Take courage! It is I, don't be afraid."** What happens next is awesome; Peter actually says, "Lord, if it's you, tell me to come to you on the water." Jesus calls him, he steps out of the boat onto the crashing waves, and as long as he keeps his eyes affixed upon the Lord, he walks on the water toward the Lord and the storm around him fades away. Only when he takes his eyes off Jesus does the storm comes into focus, consumes him, and he sinks. Jesus, being who He is, reaches out and pulls Peter to safety; God is so awesome! Unfortunately, it took a storm in my life in order to learn what Peter did that day: as long as we keep our eyes on Jesus during the storms of life, the crashing waves that surround us will fade away, and the impossible becomes possible. With Jesus, we are able to walk on the water regardless of the circumstances that surround us.

My storm was divorce.

Jacob was a man who was a controller. He connived and manipulated his way to get what he wanted. It was a generational stronghold passed down through his mother, who encouraged her son to play a trick on his father, Isaac, by pretending to be Esau. This trick led Isaac to give the family blessing to Jacob, which meant Jacob would eventually inherit the land God had promised to Abraham's seed. Jacob also learned control from his Uncle Laban, who caused Jacob to work for fourteen years to take Rachel as his lifelong mate. One must ask which was uglier in God's sight, the self-centered nature and worldliness of Esau, or the control and manipulation of Jacob?

Control is a problem for men and women. Many women use sex to control their husbands. Many men use power and force to control their wives. Control is at the core of that which is opposite the cross-self-rule. What delivers us from this fleshly nature of control? A crisis. Jacob's crisis came when he was faced with the prospect of meeting a brother who said he would kill Jacob the next time he saw him. Esau had built his own clan and was about to meet Jacob and his clan in the middle of the desert. Jacob was fearful, so he retreated. There he met a messenger from God who wrestled with him. Jacob clung to God and refused to let go of this angel. It is the place where Jacob was given a painful but necessary spiritual heart transplant. From that point on, Jacob would walk with a limp because God had to dislocate his hip in order to overcome Jacob's strong will.

God often has to "dislocate our hip" through failure and disappointment. Sometimes it is the only way He can get our attention. Our nature to control and manipulate is so strong that it takes a catastrophic event to wake us up. Yet God did not reject Jacob for these character traits. In fact, God blessed him greatly because He saw something in Jacob that pleased Him. He saw a humble and contrite heart beneath the cold and manipulative exterior of Jacob's life, and it was that trait that God needed to develop. He did this by bringing about the crisis in Jacob's life that led to total consecration.

This event was marked by Jacob getting a new name, Israel. For the first time, Jacob had a nature change, not just a habit change. What will God have to do in our lives to gain our complete consecration to His will and purposes?[xx]

Life hurts in many different ways; through disappointments, disease, loss of loved ones, betrayal, or financial disasters like losing a job. We live in a fallen and broken world, a world that aches and every one of us at some time or another will feel the hurts of life. Have you ever had a best friend betray you? Or how about the time you pulled an all-nighter studying for an important exam and still failed it? Do you know someone who has walked through the anguish of a miscarriage or an abortion? Have you ever worked diligently and faithfully at your place of work expecting a promotion and lost out to a coworker? This list is endless…

Life is not an injury-free sport.

The pain and anguish of this journey called "life" somehow seeps deep down into the recesses of our hearts and beats us down day after day. Some of us can let the tears flow and find relief while others buy into the lie that we don't feel those things.

The author of Lamentations finds himself immersed in the tragedy and pains of life. To better understand the real circumstances of that time we have to know what it was like during the final days of Jerusalem before King Nebuchadnezzar breached its walls. The days before the destruction of Jerusalem marked the fulfillment of Jeremiah's words about the coming famine, pestilence, and sword. They were dark days full of terrors and horrors.

So I say, "My splendor is gone and all that I had hoped from the LORD." I remember my affliction and my wandering, the bitterness and the gall. I well remember them, and my soul is downcast within me. Yet this I call to mind and therefore I have hope: Because of the LORD's great love we are not consumed, for his compassions never fail. They are new every morning; great is your faithfulness. I say to myself, "The LORD is my portion; therefore I will wait for him." The LORD is good to those whose hope is in him, to the one who seeks him; it is good to wait quietly for the salvation of the LORD. —Lamentations 3:18–26 (NIV)

So many times we find ourselves in the tough places in life because we choose to do things our way and simply do not listen to God. Assuming that these tough places of life begin with our failure to listen to Him, we continue down our path of self destruction and then we encounter the loving discipline of God.

We cry out, "God…HELP!"

Then God, who is always with us, is suddenly revealed through our current circumstance and we somehow come to that place where we begin to see and experience the loving, comforting warm embrace of our Heavenly Father. The outlook on life for the author of Lamentations saw God pushing him to despair before revealing joy and goodness. God loves us so much that He will not hesitate to push us into a corner to make us face the utter misery of our current circumstances because only after we've confronted our misery can we appreciate His comfort.

God doesn't want us merely to 'get through' our problems. He wants us to 'grow through' them. —Gary Oliver

Just when it looks like you are faced with an unimaginable disaster God somehow, turns our desperate situations into an opportunity to really get to know Him and His peace and joy begins to fill the atmosphere of our circumstances. It's indescribable. Many times I have found my time in the wilderness a very desolate and lonely place.

When my spirit was overwhelmed within me, then thou knewest my path. —Psalms 142:3a (KJV)

It's during these times when we feel that no one cares, and it's impossible just to get through the day, but then He comes to us. He embraces us with the warmth of His arms and comforts us with His presence. It literally surrounds and consumes us in a way that makes this temporary experience of isolation worthwhile. I once read that you can define loneliness as the surprising opportunity to really have an encounter and truly know God. The wilderness is a lonely place of discovery, a place that you will find a deep revelation of who God really is. As the darkness closes in around you, be of good cheer because there is hope beyond the night. God is here to pick you up and hold you close.

In the wilderness, He forces us to draw deep upon His grace to survive.

Remember, we will stay in the wilderness with God until He has accomplished what He wants within us. Although not at first, I have learned that the wilderness is not a place to fear, but a place that you can hear God's voice like never before. It is in the wilderness that He can reveal himself to you in awesome ways. It is here that your intimacy with Him grows. It is here where the rushing wind of the Spirit of God will smash the idols in your life and cast out all of your foes. It is here you will experience the spectacular reality of the one true living God and you will see that He is a loving God that so desires a relationship with you!

Remember every road that GOD led you on for those forty years in the wilderness, pushing you to your limits, testing you so that he would know what you were made of, whether you would keep his commandments or not. —Deuteronomy 8:2 (MSG)

Written in the pages of the book of Hosea, God would lead Israel out into the wilderness and court her far away from all of the distractions so He could speak clearly to His children. Even though His people went astray to worship other idols, in His great mercy He spoke tenderly to His people wanting to restore His relationship with them and to change what had been a time of great difficulty into a day of hope.

This winepress of God is designed to make us more Christ-like, to make us a mirror reflection of His Son. He wants to ripen within us the fruit of the Spirit: love, joy, peace, patience, kindness, goodness, faithfulness, gentleness, self-control. I began to realize that one way He accomplishes this is by putting us into situations that are completely opposite of the fruit He is trying to ripen. I also discovered that more often than not, one's suffering and brokenness amplifies our helplessness and truly exposes our need for a Savior. Jesus, when He later spoke with the formerly blind man, described His mission this way: *"For judgment I came into this world, that those who do not see may see; and that those who see may become blind." —John 9:39 (KJV)*

Knees

Each and every one of us are beautifully woven together in our mother's womb by a loving God, but for some reason, many of us lose our way to hatred and make the decision to go it alone. The good news is that God's love for us is so great that He will take extreme measures to gain our attention to pursue our hearts, because He is a God of redemption. In fact, the whole Bible account is a story of redemption. When you cross paths with people who have lost their way to hate, do not fear their arrogance, instead see them as God sees them—people who desperately need a Savior.

We've all heard the saying at some point in our life, "The bigger they are, the harder they fall," and in many cases it turns out to be true. God has called many hard-headed and hard-hearted people into His Kingdom miraculously by rescuing them from the desperate pit of their circumstances. You may have heard or read something very similar to this:

> Noah was drunk, Abraham was too old, Isaac was a daydreamer, Jacob was a liar, Joseph was abused, Moses was a murderer (like David and Paul), Gideon was afraid, Rahab was a prostitute, Jeremiah and Timothy were too young, David pretended to be mad, had an affair and ran away from his own son, Elijah was suicidal, Jonah ran away from God, Naomi was a widow, Job was bankrupt, John the Baptist ate locusts, Peter was impulsive and hot-tempered, John was self-righteous, The disciples fell asleep while praying, Martha worried about everything, Mary was so Jesus minded she was no earthly good, Mary Magdalene was demon-possessed, The boy with the fish and five rolls of bread was too unknown (and still is), The Samaritan woman was divorced—more than once, Zacchaeus was too small, Paul was too religious, Timothy had a stomach ulcer, and Lazarus was dead. —Author Unknown

God gave them all a new heart and transformed them. Do not let the exterior of people fool you; we are needy people who are desperately crying out for help and I was one of them!

"Don't be afraid, I've redeemed you. I've called your name. You're mine. When you're in over your head, I'll be there with you. When you're in rough waters, you will not go down. When you're between a rock and a hard place, it won't be a dead end -- Because I am GOD, your personal God, The Holy of Israel, your Savior. I paid a huge price for you...That's how much you mean to me! That's how much I love you! I'd sell off the whole world to get you back, trade the creation just for you. —Isaiah 43:1–4 (MSG)

I walked through dark and desperate places of living life my own way, only to find myself in a condition of complete depravity, loneliness, and shame. My desperate circumstances eventually eroded away enough of "self" to bring me to my knees in surrender. These moments are when God loves to jump in with His grace and pierce your midnight with a brilliant sunshine only experienced by the forgiven and redeemed. Through His love, mercy, and incredible grace, He is raising me up. He brings us life through His death and there is no greater love than this!

That's why we can be so sure that every detail in our lives of love for God is worked into something good. - Romans 8:28 (MSG)

I have discovered in the pages of God's word that people such as Moses, Joseph and David needed to symbolically seize four significant stones or building blocks (Walls, Mountains, Wilderness, and Promised Land) before they were ready to step into their God-given destiny. God had to deal with their walls before they could see the vision He had for them on the mountaintop, which provided the survival catalyst in the wilderness, which eventually would lead them to victory in the Promised Land.

God has a way of taking all of our stuff, choices, mistakes, and tragedies and weaves them together into His perfect will for our lives, but first we must surrender ourselves to Him. I was starting to understand who I was. It was at my place of surrender where He began the process of renewing my spirit and setting my heart free—I did not have to be a captive anymore.

I wanted to trust Him.

I wanted to abandon myself to Him.

I wanted to just belong to Him.

Behold, I will do a new thing; now it shall spring forth; shall ye not know it? I will even make a way in the wilderness, and rivers in the desert. —Isaiah 43:19 (KJV)

…I fell to my knees.

Jars

His holiness, His majesty, and His endless love somehow penetrate deep into our core, exposing our condition. Standing before Him in all of my shame and brokenness, I began to tremble. Tears of sorrow anoint His feet like a heavy spring rain as I collapsed under the heaviness of His presence. With a broken whisper, I barley spoke the words, "Lord, please…please…I need You to love me!"

He gently reaches down and begins catching my tears in His wounded hands. The smile on His face and the gentleness in His eyes pierce through my brokenness as His grace begins to calm my trembling. Then it happens, the moment I have been waiting for all of my life—He lifts me to my feet and hugs me. Lost in His embrace my tears of shame and sorrow become tears of joy. He is the God who has everything and I found it amazing that He wanted me. He would hold me for hours and tell me over and over again how much He loved me!

"What kind of grace is this?"

I discovered in the wilderness that the Samaritan woman at the well symbolizes all of us who have used their best efforts to satisfy the yearning for love and completion. She had five failed marriages (I had two), lived in guilt and shame and intentionally avoided everyone because of the rejection she was carrying. Seemingly out of nowhere, Jesus walks onto the scene and asks her for a drink and she debates Him. This sound so familiar, doesn't it?

This is brilliant—Jesus responds, **"If you only knew…"** What is He really getting at here? He is inviting us to give Him all the stuff that keeps us thirsting in life, because what He has is better. In the case of the Samaritan woman, every time she jumps into another relationship, she thinks it will satisfy her, but it doesn't. What is it for you?

He offers Himself to be the completer of her life and yours. She debates Him when He asks for a drink. How many times has Jesus asked you for a drink and you respond with debate? How many times have you been in failed, broken situations over and over again? Her situation was five failed marriages. Maybe this is not you, but there are probably five failed things in your life that have left you thirsty over and over again.

The woman at the well desperately journeyed through life searching for her heart's true desire never finding it. Like the woman at the well, we don't understand that we are trying to fill a void in our lives that can only be filled by God. Jesus cuts to the core of our pain because no matter how many relationships we have or how much money we have or how many possessions we have or whatever the case may be—if we don't have Christ, we will always be thirsty. Nothing the world has to offer will quench this thirst, but when we invite Jesus into the details of our lives, the thirst will be quenched with living water. If we choose not to acknowledge this void we have in our hearts, like the Samaritan woman, we too will make many lonely trips to well of our disappointments carrying our jars of brokenness. Here is the awesome part of this scene—she did not set the appointment, God did!

He is the God of another chance!

He is the God that pursues you!

> There is a God-shaped vacuum in the heart of every man which cannot be filled by any created thing, but only by God the Creator, made known through Jesus Christ. — Blaise Pascal

As we step into the pages of His story we find that inside every man and every woman there is a deep spiritual thirst for God Himself. We spend so much of our time living a life of quiet desperation and all of our attempts to quench or satisfy this thirst by some other means is met with dissatisfaction and fractured broken lives. It's important to understand that Jesus was not pointing out her issues and her sins to be mean and upsetting; there is a difference between guilt and conviction. Guilt is satan's (and the world's) way of bringing us down. Conviction is God's' way of bringing us up.

This woman was lonely for God and it wasn't water or a human relationship that she needed; she needed the one true living God. How about you? To have a God moment, we have to acknowledge our void. Like her, so many of us have toiled through life trying it our way and where has it really gotten us?

Here is the rub…we don't have an image issue, we have a heart issue. It's amazing the extent we go to try to hide our brokenness and failures. Somehow we believe that failure means we are weak or that we are not good enough. The world tells us that if we can avoid exposing who we really are than we can control other's perception of us. We become locked into the cycle. We don't want to be exposed, we operate out of fear and we allow pride to take root in our hearts and our real selves stay in hiding and we lose our hearts. Coming out of hiding will cost you. It will be difficult and rough at first, but it's exactly the place where God shows up and wraps His grace around us! This is where we begin to taste real freedom as the shame, hurt and failure is exposed. The process of redemption comes as our stuff is exposed.

In John 4:28 do you realize what she did? She put down the jar she was carrying and left it behind. When you have a collision with the living God, He never comes into your life to leave you where you're at. Everyone that has a pulse is carrying brokenness, wounds and baggage in our jars! Some of us are embarrassed or terrified to share what we are carrying in our jars. Only the Creator can take all the brokenness, wounds, and baggage of our fractured lives and put the pieces back together into a beautiful new creation. God begins this restoration process when we give Him the broken pieces of our hearts, which is what I did on the mountaintop that day.

Not easy at all, but there was a simplicity in setting down my jars—it freed my hands so I could run into the loving arms of my Abba, my Daddy God! Holding me close, He smiles and says, **"I promised that I would hold you when everything fell apart. It's OK my precious child, Your Daddy is here!"**

Holding me tighter, He gently sings to me, **"Your tears are My tears, and I have always been with you. I love you so much! You belong to Me, and I want you to know that I will never let you go, even** when you come undone. I made you with My own hands, and I love you more than you can imagine. Heaven holds a dream just for you; come take hold of it!"

But I'll take the hand of those who don't know the way, who can't see where they're going. I'll be a personal guide to them, directing them through unknown country. I'll be right there to show them what roads to take, make sure they don't fall into the ditch. These are the things I'll be doing for them—sticking with them, not leaving them for a minute." —Isaiah 42:16 (MSG)

Confrontation

It doesn't matter how broken you are or how desperate your situation is, God can heal you and put all the scattered pieces of your life back together. He knows your deepest needs, dreams, struggles, fears and regrets. He knows how deeply you are hurting and is desperately waiting to start the restoration process. His grace is greater than all the junk in our life, and His amazing love will overfill the deep void of all of our longings. He knows you.

Remember the movie the *Lion King*? Remember when Simba "checks out" and runs as far away as he could in the other direction? He forgot who he was. A transformation happens when Simba looks into the water, and his reflection becomes the face of his father Mufasa. Here are the words that are exchanged between father and son.

Mufasa: Simba…
Simba: Father?
Mufasa: Simba, have you forgotten me?
Simba: No! How could I?
Mufasa: You have forgotten who you are, and so forgotten me. Look inside yourself, Simba…you are more than what you have become.
Simba: How can I go back? I'm not who I used to be.
Mufasa: Remember who you are… You are my son, and the one true king. Remember who you are…[xxi]

Who I believed I was…
- I was weak
- I was easily manipulated
- I was starving for attention
- I was angry
- I was frustrated
- I was rejected
- I was unlovable

Who I really am…
- I am strong
- I have purpose
- I am a good father
- I am not controlled by my past
- I am anticipating a victorious future
- I will live in advance of security
- I will not compromise
- I am not afraid
- I am lovable and loved
- I have integrity
- I have good character

At the crossroads of the wilderness and the Promised Land, the Lord began changing my perspective. This was the place where He gave me a new name:

"My precious child, you will no longer be called broken, alone or afraid. Today I bless you with a new name…Redeemed. Remember, you are MINE!"

The winds were beginning to change and the grace of God gave me the gift of another chance. Self-reproach is a condition of deep regret or blaming yourself for a fault or a mistake. Simba struggled with this and so did I. Tough part is that we tend to get stuck here and not move forward.

> We are all under the same mental calamity; we have all forgotten our names. We have all forgotten what we really are. — G.K. Chesterton

I invite you to check out the book of Job starting at chapter 38, where Job steps into the ring with God regarding his circumstances. Although we may not have suffered to the same extent as Job, we all have to ask ourselves this piercing question, "Are we worse off than Job or more righteous than Job?" God is in control despite what our circumstances tell us and we have to learn the "simple to understand but difficult to apply" lesson that we need to give God a chance to reveal His greater purpose for us. This purpose may unfold over the course of our lives and not necessarily on our timeline. When we allow ourselves to gain another perspective of the book of Job, we can begin to see that this incredible book is intimately connected to the New Testament because all of Job's questions and problems are perfectly answered in Jesus Christ.

This journey is teaching me that milestones will emerge in life for the purpose of inviting us to change our perspective. For instance—when you begin to understand that God is with you in all your circumstances, when you begin to understand that God has a purpose for the storms we go through in life or we are puzzled by God's response to our question because He responds to the question behind the question. Tough stuff!

These milestones became places of confrontation.

It was one of those autumn days in New England where the temperature hung around 50 degrees Fahrenheit, and the blue sky was mixed with swirls of white puffy clouds. A day where you couldn't escape those familiar autumn smells and the sight of brilliantly colored leaves dancing across the ground, whisked along by the invisible hands of a cool breeze, reminding you that the season wasn't ready to surrender into winter's grip. This picture perfect day was interrupted when my ex-wife called to verbally rip me a new one. Arriving to my boiling point, I hung up and threw the phone across the room.

Later that night I sat in front of my computer ready to begin the e-mail joust. With a day's worth of anger consuming me, I easily composed an e-mail filled with accusatory and stinging words. With my finger hovering above the mouse button to hit send, I hesitated…something spoke to my heart telling me not to send it.

The next day on my way to work, still frustrated, I popped in a CD and listened to a message called "Resting in Father's Embrace" from Jack Frost of Shiloh Place Ministries, hoping for a distraction from my long commute. It didn't take very long into the message to for my eyes to well up with tears. What captured my attention was the narrative of Dick and Rick Hoyt. The story begins in the spring of 1977, where Rick Hoyt, who was a quadriplegic with cerebral palsy, shared with his dad that he wanted to take part in a five-mile race. Dick Hoyt, who was not even close to being a long-distance runner agreed. He ran behind his son pushing him in his wheelchair finishing the race next to last. The real victory was what Rick told his father that night, "Dad, when I'm running, it feels like I'm not handicapped." Wow!

Rick Hoyt was set free of his handicap that day, while I was letting the failure of my marriage and growing anger handicap me. I had to win. I had to be right. I lost sight. God used this story to show me that I didn't have to win or to be right. He exposed my true motivation of wanting to send the email. Later that day He spoke these words to my heart in my devotional time with Him.

"Beloved, the enemy is trying to separate you from others by establishing rejection through misunderstanding and offense. Don't take the bait! Forgive everything that puts you on the defensive. Develop a generous attitude toward others by giving them the benefit of the doubt, regardless of the situation. You can choose to win this spiritual battle with a Godly attitude. I will take care of this. I am well prepared to defend you. What I allow to be removed, I will restore, and if not in this lifetime, the next. Your part is blessing—not cursing those who come against you. Let Me defend your honor. I know the final chapter of your life because I wrote it, says the Lord"

I made a choice to not take the bait.

I deleted the e-mail.

Thank you God.

Even though I didn't like the words from my ex-wife, I needed to let go it go and surrender it to God. He helped me see the self-reproach and the fears in my own life. The reality—I was just as guilty at times of initiating a round of verbal jousting with my ex-wife too. I would get caught up in a power play of trying justify how much more right I was than her and never yielding.

Goliath came at King Saul and the armies of Israel so hard that he paralyzed them with fear and panic. Then into this wild scene walks a shepherd boy named David, who didn't tremble or run from the taunts of this giant. David saw the giant he was facing through the eyes of God, which changed his perspective. We can learn from this confrontation that David did not weigh the risk of failure because his faith was resting totally in the living God. In God, there is no real failure when we act.

Court, intimidation, financial problems, and tragedy after tragedy were some of the training grounds the Lord used to teach me to confront my fears head on. I began to understand that the giants I faced on this journey did their best to intimidate me, but I would learn that these were merely tactics of the enemy designed to keep me in fear. These lessons on the battlefield of life are sharpening my faith and building my trust in the Lord no matter what circumstances come my way. I read in a study of Matthew 6:34 that fear robs us of our today, our tomorrow and gives victory to our past.

One of the greatest tests that we will face along this journey of life is can we trust in God's goodness even though life does not make sense at times? This involves a change in perspective where we must learn to trust in God who is good and not always the goodness of life!

Does my faithfulness to my convictions really do any good at all?

As I dive deeper into His word, the more I see that God is still concerned with every situation that I face even though He doesn't intervene immediately. God will have the final say and the day is coming when He will settle all accounts. In a broad scope of time, God executes His justice, and we have His promise to this very fact in His word. We must overcome our desire to give up and not lose hope.

I'm learning that it's so much easier to run into the headwinds of life when I ask God to run the race with me than going it alone. As my perspective started changing, it happens...I look down at the water's surface and begin to see the faint reflection of my Heavenly Father. What is really happening here? God is telling me that I have what it takes and that I am adored. This is played out in a snippet from the movie, The Matrix...check it out.

Trinity: What is he doing?!
Morpheus: He's beginning to believe...[xxii]

Now I can say to my heavenly Father, "Dad, when I'm running with You, it feels like I'm not handicapped."

Nightsong

Wandering through life with a vain pursuit of self, circumstances eventually hunted me down and forced me to look into the mirror of myself. Standing in front of the mirror, with a tear running down my face, it took everything I had to see the stranger looking back at me. I became a person that I knew deep down inside I wasn't, but I didn't have the courage to come out of hiding. Numbing myself to the pain in life, I convinced myself that it was easier to exist behind a mask, paralyzed at the thought of being exposed. I exhausted myself trying to outrun my pain. This is not who I wanted to be. I was living life the way I wanted to live it, but once my eyes were opened, I realized that I wasn't free. Flying solo in life left me tired, beaten down, and empty. I've tried so long to make it on my own that my hopes and dreams became scattered fragments of what they could have been.

> The strength of a ship is only fully demonstrated when it faces a hurricane, and the power of the gospel can only be fully exhibited when a Christian is subjected to some fiery trial. We must understand that for God to give "songs in the night," He must first make it night. —Nathaniel William Taylor

Sometimes there is no way out of your circumstances than to completely trust God. Sometimes He will not allow things to go your way, because He loves you. Is your night one of discouragement, rejection, or failure? Do you feel that no one understands you? Take heart, your Father in heaven will come near to you in the night and give you a song—a song of hope, which will be harmonious with the strong, resonant music of His amazing grace and providence. There is freedom waiting in the sweet rhythm of His song.

"Why are you looking for love? Why are you still searching as if I'm not enough? Tell me where will you run? At the point of your breaking I'll be there waiting for you. I am the God who loves you, who sees you struggling, who hears your

cries, who calls you by name, who overcomes your failures, who pursues you, who can sustain you through all your fears and doubts. Beloved, come out of hiding—stop trying to outrun your past and stop trying to outrun Me."

Let me share a truth I learned—pain has a way of revealing our weakness and will draw us toward Him if we allow it. I've never been closer to God than through the pain I went through. I'm not saying that God causes hopeless situations in your life; the reality is that there are lots of reasons why bad things happen. Much of the heartache we experience just comes from living in a broken world filled with broken people. Another big reason is that we are human and have the capacity to make some very stupid choices along the way. From my experiences, I've learned that God will allow pain and unexpected crisis in order to detach you from hope and everything else and attach it only to Himself.

> God whispers to us in our pleasures, speaks to us in our conscience, but shouts in our pains: It is His megaphone to rouse a deaf world. —C. S. Lewis

I was consumed in justifying myself apart from God, and it left me worn out, tired, and empty. Every day, I would run as hard as I could trying to find value and worth in everything else but where it was all the time—in God. I looked for it in the approval of my father, my mother, in others, in two marriages, in money, in achievement, in position and in power…I'm sure there are more places.

I spent so much time pursuing acceptance in these places that I lost everything that mattered. I became the sum total of all the expectations that I placed on my life giving up my identity, my true self just to belong. I discovered that many of the places I looked for love and acceptance never truly accepted or loved me back. What I did discover in the journey out of the midnight of my soul was that loving God is what my heart desired and what's really awesome—He accepts me for who I am and…loves me back.

I didn't deliberately decide to erode my marriage by being distant. I didn't deliberately make stupid, destructive choices that cost me my dreams and ruined everything I had worked for. The tough reality is that I drifted away from my God-inspired life, and I didn't even know it because I was so lost. Once I came to the end of myself, I wrestled with the humiliation of knowing I couldn't get back on my own. God knew that we couldn't save ourselves. He knew we needed someone to rescue us and bring us back home. That's why God stepped into human history.

Some major storms had to happen in my life for me to get past "myself." It was in that place where I was asked the piercing question, **"Are you going to rise up and become the man of God I created you to be or are you going to keep running?"** He showed me that I didn't have to be the petty, deceitful, lying, manipulative, greedy, self-centered, driven, people-pleasing fool anymore. This was not who I was nor is it the legacy He wanted me to leave behind. The meaning, approval and purpose I was desperately seeking, was right in front of me the whole time and I almost missed it. No matter how hard I strived in my own efforts, I couldn't find what I was looking. My value and worth could only be found in the blessing and grace of God Himself.

When you're desperate for grace and you've messed your life up beyond your ability to fix it, the "Christian" rules you knew and the ones you've lived by won't make sense anymore.

Let go and fall into His arms.

He is the author of your past, present, and your future. Don't let the enemy of your heart convince you that you had too many failures, lost too many battles, or messed up beyond God's loving reach. Your dreams are still alive in the heart of your heavenly Father. Let Him bring those dreams back to life in you. Let Him show you the life He has planned for you. At some point, you have to move away from the perspective that God is trying to do something to you and step into the reality that He is trying to do something in you or through you. Here is a question to wrap yourself around: why is that we trust God with our eternity, but not with our today or our tomorrow?

Please get this: the storms will come and winds will blow in your life, but it's not here where I've found my hope. My beating heart, my very soul is held by the One who won't ever let me go…and so I'll cling to my God! You know, the amazing thing about God is that He knows us and loves us anyway. The greatest enemy of trust is fear. Trust Him. The more we try to control others and things around us, the more frustration, anxiety, and unrealized potential we invite into our lives. As long as we are aware of how little control we have, we begin to have a healthy perspective. The more we try to reach for control in our lives, the harder things become. He wants you to attach your hope only to Him!

If my scars could speak, they would cry out and tell you that it was only His incredibly love and grace that made all my shadows disappear. When you come to the place where you're broken, that's where the healing begins. It's the very place where God's radical grace collides with your circumstances. The reality is that no matter how dark, hopeless, or painful your situation is, we have a God who can take the worst and turn it into something good.

Expect the dawn of a new beginning in the dark nights of life.
—Lloyd John Ogilvie

Remember, your circumstances are not your god; God is your God!

Psalms 73 [My Version]

God is so good, but I allowed the culture and the lies of the world to dull my senses and blind me over time so I almost missed seeing His goodness. I foolishly took my eyes off Him and became intoxicated by people in high places, envying the success of those who have made it to the top and desperately seeking this to define my own identity. I believed that these people worried about nothing, and their status and wealth provided them with the comfort of not having a care in the world.

What I couldn't see beneath the veil was their conceit and arrogance, how selfish they were at the core, their uncaring hearts, their aggressively doing whatever it took for them to get what they wanted with no regard for others, their evil conceit that knew no limits, their being friendly to your face and mocking you to others behind your back. In their arrogance, they would threaten oppression and destroy the peace. People actually listened to them—I actually listened to them—can you believe it?

What's going on? God, where are You? Can't You see what's going on down here? God, why do I suffer though I live for You? Why do those who deny You have it better than I do? Everywhere I looked I felt the sorrow and the pain of empty living. This is giving me a headache…

In the blink of an eye, disaster! Reaching the end of myself through crisis, I ran into the loving arms of God and He began to show me the whole picture: searching for love, I continued to reach out for the things that kept destroying me. A blind curve on a dark road—a living nightmare! I would wake up and see nothing—nothing! I am so sick of envying the lives of so many I see, somehow believing that they have what I need. I spent my life focusing on a score that I could never win.

Lord, please cover my eyes so that my heart can finally see that when it's all said and done, You are the only thing that means anything. God, You are enough for me! Lord, how refreshing it is to be in Your presence. God, I am coming home to You and telling the world what You did for me.

> My heart may fail, but the Lord is the strength of my heart and my portion forever.

> He is my heartstone!

Hope

Having a right set of doctrines is not enough. This truth was put to the test in the trials and storms of my journey, and it drove me beyond my superficial acceptance of the truth into a deeper understanding of God's very nature.

Did you know that the core of Christianity is not a set of philosophies, a religion, a world view, or even the teachings of Jesus? It's the resurrection of Jesus Christ. Jesus is alive and He cleared the way for us to have an intimate relationship with the living God. We spend a lifetime in hopeless pursuit of everything else expect God, ignoring that the very heart-cry of our soul is for a relationship with Him.

We tend by a secret law of the soul to move toward our mental image of God. —A. W. Tozer

Do you have a clear and accurate picture of who God really is?

Do you really know God? Do you?

Everything hinges on who you envision God to be.

He is not some distant, shallow, narcissistic, judgmental, killjoy in the sky. God loves us more than we could ever imagine and He is passionately committed to us. Life, technology, busyness and so many other things get in the way of this pursuit and we become so distracted that one day we find ourselves leading a life of 'quiet desperation'. We must not be distracted on our journey into the very nature of God. His heart cries out, **"You turned your back on Me, but I'm not turning My back on you. You have no idea what I will do to get you back my child."** God's passion to redeem us by stepping into our world and dying for us isn't because of anything we have done or could ever do—it's only because of His amazing grace. It doesn't matter what we've done or haven't done, He still offers us grace. God pursues us, God accepts us completely, and despite how messed up we are, He provides a way back to Him. "I love you" could not have been said a better way!

Do you believe that God has already written your story and all you have to do is let go, take hold of your destiny moment and step into the pages of His story? Philippians 1:6 tells us tells us that God finishes what He begins, but we need to take the first step and jump into what He has written for our lives.

Are you worn out?

Are you broken?

Are you fractured?

Are you desperate?

Are you ready to give up?

Are you hopeless?

There is hope for the brokenness and it's a portrait of grace that can heal all of life's heartaches and pain—it's Jesus Christ! Our Heavenly Father gave us His Son to go to the cross for us! Swallow your foolish pride, stop believing the lies, and bring all the fractured and broken pieces of your life to Him. The God of relationship will surround you with His redemptive love and grace, and He will restore your broken lives and heart to His. Beloved, He loves you so much!

May the God of hope fill you with all joy and peace as you trust in him, so that you may overflow with hope by the power of the Holy Spirit. —Romans 15:13 (NIV)

I don't know how turbulent your life is at this very moment or how deep your pain is, but I do know that God is bigger than all of it. He is big enough to take all of the pain, fear, anger and the stuff of your life that you can throw at Him and love you through it all. He never promised us that we'll be exempt from the trials and tribulations of life, but He does promise that when everything comes crashing down around you—you will be held by His grace.

We all need to know we are held. We all need to know that someone realizes life is too short and that we feel as if we are falling through the cracks. His word is a love story with a consistent theme of hope! No matter how miserable your current circumstances are or how big your giants are or how many your sins are…God offers hope for a brighter tomorrow.

Christ's life showed me how, and enabled me to do it. I identified myself completely with him. Indeed, I have been crucified with Christ. My ego is no longer central. It is no longer important that I appear righteous before you or have your good opinion, and I am no longer driven to impress God. Christ lives in me. The life you see me living is not "mine," but it is lived by faith in the Son of God, who loved me and gave himself for me. I am not going to go back on that. Is it not clear to you that to go back to that old rule-keeping, peer-pleasing religion would be an abandonment of everything personal and free in my relationship with God? I refuse to do that, to repudiate God's grace. If a living relationship with God could come by rule-keeping, then Christ died unnecessarily. —Galatians 2:20, 21 (MSG)

From my own journey, I can tell you that every storm will start with just a drop of rain, a single tear, but if our hope is in the Lord…it changes everything.

Tears

Today the illusions of this world around me fade away.
I do not want to be afraid…
When our eyes meet, I know I am safe.
Have I been orphaned, fallen within this blind dismay?
Through the silence of night His glory invades, scatters my gray.
This child runs to You!

Cold and alone, His breath brings to life emptiness inside.

I do not want to be afraid…
When our eyes meet, I know I am safe.
These tears paint the scene of my face, still sore and dried.
These tears scar my sorrow from this lullaby of pain.
"Release your dreams to Me on the winds of change, your past lay aside'
'Run to Me my child!'"

Hands outstretched, my life redeemed, held by His grace.
Glory scatters the fear, I am not afraid!
When our eyes meet, I know I am safe.
Soaring upon wings of eagles, held by hope I see His face.
Captured within this vision of joy, I run to His embrace.

"My Child, my beloved, I am here with you…Run for me!"

These tears of joy from my Abba, I catch within my hands.
Made new and cleansed by His gentle healing rains,
Through the fire and whatever the cost, I will be with Him forever.
Tears of shame and fear restored to tears of joy, He understands.
I have found the way and now I run for Him!

I do not walk this road of tears alone!

Those who sow in tears will reap with songs of joy. He who goes out weeping, carrying seed to sow, will return with songs of joy, carrying sheaves with him. —Psalms 126:5, 6 (NIV)

God is telling us that if our hope is in Him during these circumstances, He will turn our tears into joy. When we find ourselves in the tear-filled sorrows of life's storms, our tendency is to run to our hiding places of fear and hurt. It is during this time when the enemy's footholds of unbelief, hopelessness and self-pity consume our thoughts that there is no way out. Remember, there is a way out and there is hope!

We can come out of our hiding places and find a place of grace with all our imperfections, so the life He has given to each of us can be released! Come out from under all the weight of your mistakes and open up your broken heart to Him, release your life to Him. He became broken for you and no one knows how to love more than He does. He can put all the broken pieces of your life, of your heart back in place and shine reflections of forgiveness upon you. He can take all of your mistakes, every scar, and every tear and redeem it into something beautiful!

I was lost within the hopelessness of an empty heart and was crushed by chains of shame, but His awesome love, forgiveness, and grace set me free. All my pain, all my shame, and all of my tears have been wiped away! His hands of love touched and healed my broken life! The sun is shining again, my story is being rewritten, and all my dreams can now come true. It's time to leave the past behind and walk with Him into a new beginning.

The trials of life can bring a heart to the abyss of despair, creating an emotional and spiritual death at our core. The brokenness of my heart was not the stinging pain of loneliness and hurt as much as it was the harsh energies of bitterness, anger, and hatred. Sadly, my heart became more and more broken over time and I somehow lost the joy of life. Truth be told, sometimes I imagined the pain of death more manageable than the perpetual shredding of my heart. But in order to stand amid the battle, we must fight to keep all the pain from turning into a voracious cancer that destroys the heart and prevents us from loving well.

My hope was found in the wonderful, loving God, who walked with me, held me, gave me the courage to face my pain, and offered a promise that resulted in a transformed heart and a joy that overwhelmed the midnight of my soul like a sunrise scattering the darkness. What the enemy could not take from me was hope. The enemy had lost the battle.

The thief comes only to steal and kill and destroy; I have come that they may have life, and have it to the full." —John 10:10 (NIV)

I found my life in Him.

I have never felt anything like the love of Jesus. Ever.

For all that I thought was hopeless in this life, the uncertainty of my future, this long road ahead looks wonderful because I know without hesitation or doubt that I am held by grace!

I run in the path of your commandments, for you have set my heart free —Psalm 119:32 (WEB)

Lift up all the broken pieces of your life to Him.

Lift them up to the God of love.

Lift them up to the God of peace.

Lift them up to the God of mercy.

Lift them up to the God of forgiveness.

Lift them up to the God of freedom.

Lift them up to the God of hope.

Lift them up to the God of grace.

Lift up your hearts.

Above all else, guard your heart, for it is the wellspring of life. —Proverbs 4:23 (NIV)

As much as I tried, I could never get home with a broken heart. It was in the midnight of my soul that He came to carry me home—held by grace. I still don't have all the answers, but I have experienced the life changing presence of the living God through Jesus Christ and that has changed everything for me—it has given me life! The words of William Wallace echo true, "Every man dies. Not every man really lives."

Lift up the broken pieces of your heart to Him and let him carry you home too! Praise to You Almighty and gracious Father. You have given me hope when there was none. You have given me strength when my resolve was gone. You have blessed me with grace and poured Your love into my heart. For your love, forgiveness and grace, I praise You. In Jesus' name. Amen.

Remember

My eyes opened slowly as I was pulled into the conversation of the chickens and roosters cackling away from the barn across the street. I looked out the bedroom window and was greeted by the warm embrace of the summer morning sunshine as it and the warm breeze invaded the room, seeming to dance with one another in the curtains. I would pause and listen to the engaging melodies of the birds enjoying the gift of this new day and watched them flutter by the window with a childlike freedom. Remembering that June had unleashed a torrent of rainfall for almost the entire month, I welcomed the warm bright serenity of this July morning.

Not wanting this moment to escape me, I stayed in bed and got lost in the wonderful sights, sounds, and smells of God's beautiful creation. Soaking in it, my thoughts began to wander as I remembered hiking up Mt. Lafayette last year with my father. I am still amazed at the incredible gift that God gave me on that hike—the gift of a heartstone. I then began to recall the four stones, my wilderness experience, and all the other wonderful adventures I have gone on with God—journeying with Him though my walls, over my mountains, into my wilderness, and into His Promised Land. God taught me many things through these adventures, but a significant place of healing was discovering that even in my brokenness He loves me apart from my performance. Discovering this created such devotion and a gratitude toward Him that will be etched upon my heart forever.

Time has passed since walking through divorce, and although life still has its challenges I now find it easier inviting the Lord into the details of my life as I am learning to trust Him more. Arriving at the edge of my Promised Land, He is restoring my heart, my trust in Him and I am finding it easier to live in His peace. My kids are doing well, I have become friends with my ex-wife (their mom—first marriage), and we are working together as a team to co-parent our kids. Oh, and I don't want to forget to share this with you…He blessed me with a home—just some of my gifts from a loving Heavenly Father.

Knowing that this beautiful day was inviting me into adventure, it was time to get out of the soft comfort of the bed and get ready. I would continue to replay the memories over these past years as I showered and shaved, eventually grabbing a pair of shorts and short-sleeved shirt that I had laid out the night before to wear. Fumbling with my shirt as I walked over to my to get my phone, the heartstone caught my eyes. It peeked through my keys, papers, and all the other stuff we men collect on our dressers, as if I needed a morning greeting from it as well.

Smiling, I reached into the clutter on my dresser and picked up the heartstone. Holding it, I was brought back to the place in God's story when He brought the Israelites right to the very edge of the Promised Land. The story tells us of a land flowing with milk and honey, flourishing, green hills, flowing rivers and the abundance of fruits, such as pomegranates, figs and a cluster of grapes so large, two men had to carry it. As their excitement of entering into the Promised Land began to build, He warned them about forgetting Him in their new prosperity. Remember, they spent years wandering around in the wilderness completely dependent upon God for everything before arriving to this place. The greatest worship comes from a heart of gratitude and love, not out of a life of need.

But watch out! Be careful never to forget what you yourself have seen. Do not let these memories escape from your mind as long as you live! And be sure to pass them on to your children and grandchildren. —Deuteronomy 4:9 (NLT)

Holding the heartstone in my hand, God whispered to my heart, **"Don't forget Me."**

This heartstone is really nothing in itself except a simple stone, but it is a symbol and reminder of where I have been, where I am, where God has brought me from and what He is doing now in my life. God is so good. As I continue to journey through life in worshipful relationship with Him, I am not exempt from life's challenges, but now I live in the confidence that God is with me no matter what.

What story is your life telling? My story, like the heartstone on my dresser, is simple…God can take the clutter of my life with everything seemingly stacked against me and redeem it. I have learned along the way on my journey that, God isn't bound by our mistakes—we make choices and God shows up and meets us there. The truth is that we adjust ourselves to meet the will of God, not the other way around. Life is tough, really tough, but God promises to walk it out with us, and it's not over until it's over. Remember Paul? He fought until the very end.

My story is not finished and your story is not finished, but we all have a story to tell so don't try to escape life—live it with purpose. God wants you to have a beautiful ending!

Love is calling out to you—the broken!

Alone, I stand broken.

An empty heart.

Desperate for grace,

Desperate for love.

Awake in this nightmare,

I know how hopeless feels!

http://heartstonejourney.com

Notes

i Brennan Manning, *"Abba's Child"* (Colorado Springs, CO: Navpress, 1994, 2002), back cover. Used by permission.

ii http://en.wikipedia.org/wiki/Wall.

iii Mark 7:21–23

iv Proverbs 16:5

v Bill Crowder, *Joseph: Overcoming Life's Challenges* Grand Rapids, MI: RBC Ministries. © 1998. Reprinted by permission. All rights reserved.

vi Jack Frost, The Shepherd's Song: "When We Strive, God Waits. When We Rest, God Acts," Shiloh Place Ministries Newsletter, 3rd Quarter (2006), 1: http://www.shilohplace.org. Used by permission.

vii Bob Benson, *"See You at the House"* (Nashville, TN: Generoux 1986), 40. Used by permission.

viii Stormie Omartian, *The Power of a Praying® Husband* (Eugene, OR: Harvest House Publishers, 2001), 191. Copyright © 2001 by Stormie Omartian, www.harvesthousepublishers.com. Used by Permission.

ix "Morpheus' Proposal / The Real World," *The Matrix,* directed by Andy and Larry Wachowski. (Burbank, CA: Warner Bros. Pictures, 1999), DVD.

x Used by permission Excerpt taken from *The Love Dare* by Stephen Kendrick and Alex Kendrick c 2008 B&H Publishing Group

xi Thomas Merton, *New Seeds of Contemplation*, (New York: New Directions, 1961), 72.

xii Jack and Tricia Frost, "The Ministry of Restitution," Shiloh Place Ministries, Inc. http://www.shilohplace.org. Used by permission.

xiii ©Russell Kelfer. Used by permission

xiv Pastor Greg Laurie, "The Greatest Life," Devotional, 2005. Used by permission from Harvest Ministries with Greg Laurie, PO Box 4000, Riverside, CA 92514.

xv Pastor Greg Laurie, "Adjust Your Sails," Harvest Daily Devotional, 2009. Used by permission from Harvest Ministries with Greg Laurie, PO Box 4000, Riverside, CA 92514.

xvi *TGIF Today God Is First* Volume 1, "The Purpose of the Desert." Reprinted by permission from the author. Os Hillman is an international speaker and author of more than 10 books on workplace calling. To learn more, visit http://www.MarketplaceLeaders.org"

xvii *TGIF Today God Is First* Volume 1, "No More Reproach" by Os Hillman." Reprinted by permission from the author. Os Hillman is an international speaker and author of more than 10 books on workplace calling. To learn more, visit http://www.MarketplaceLeaders.org"

xviii http://en.wikipedia.org/wiki/Stone_of_Scone.

xix "The Black Gate Opens," The Return of the King, directed by Peter Jackson (New Line Home Entertainment, A Time Warner Company, 2004), DVD.

xx *TGIF Today God Is First* Volume 1, "Wrestling with God" by Os Hillman." Reprinted by permission from the author. Os Hillman is an international speaker and author of more than 10 books on workplace calling. To learn more, visit http://www.MarketplaceLeaders.org"

xxi "Mufasa's Ghost," *The Lion King,* directed by Roger Allers and Rob Minkoff (Anahiem, CA: Disney, 1994), DVD.

xxii "Subway Showdown," *The Matrix,* directed by Andy and Larry Wachowski. (Burbank, CA: Warner Bros. Pictures, 1999), DVD.

Made in the USA
Lexington, KY
18 August 2011